T0340335

Writing a Business Plan

Resourcing new ventures is all-important for entrepreneurs, and creating a successful business plan can be make or break when it comes to attracting investment. Written by an experienced academic and consultant, this book provides a concise guide for producing the optimal business plan.

Business plans are vital when it comes to making strategic decisions and monitoring progress. *Writing a Business Plan* is designed to teach you how to write your business plan without relying on someone else or internet templates. It will take you through each stage of business-plan writing, with chapters on generating ideas; describing business opportunities; drawing a business road map; and considering marketing, financial, operations, HR, legal and risk. The book includes a range of features to assist you, including worked-through examples.

This unique book provides a one-stop shop for entrepreneurs and students of entrepreneurship to hone their skills in writing a useful and comprehensive business plan.

Ignatius Ekanem is Senior Lecturer in Business Management at Middlesex University Business School, London. Dr Ekanem specializes in economic regeneration and small-business research, with particular focus on the financial management practices of small and medium-sized businesses.

Routledge Focus on Business and Management

The fields of business and management have grown exponentially as areas of research and education. This growth presents challenges for readers trying to keep up with the latest important insights. Routledge Focus on Business and Management presents small books on big topics and how they intersect with the world of business.

Individually, each title in the series provides coverage of a key academic topic, whilst, collectively, the series forms a comprehensive collection across the business disciplines.

ISSN: 2475–6369

For a complete list of titles in this series, please visit www.routledge.com/business/series/FBM.

Writing a Business Plan
A Practical Guide

Ignatius Ekanem

Routledge
Taylor & Francis Group

LONDON AND NEW YORK

First published 2017
by Routledge
2 Park Square, Milton Park, Abingdon, Oxon OX14 4RN

and by Routledge
605 Third Avenue, New York, NY 10017

First issued in paperback 2021

Routledge is an imprint of the Taylor & Francis Group, an informa business

British Library Cataloguing-in-Publication Data
A catalogue record for this book is available from the British Library

Library of Congress Cataloging-in-Publication Data
A catalog record for this book has been requested

ISBN 13: 978-0-367-78817-9 (pbk)
ISBN 13: 978-1-138-20602-1 (hbk)

Typeset in Times New Roman
by Apex CoVantage, LLC

Write the vision and make it plain on tablets, that he may run who reads it.

(Habakkuk 2:2)

To Ekemini, Edidiong and Etieno

Contents

Illustrations

About the author

Dr Ignatius Ekanem holds a PhD in Financial Management of SMEs from Middlesex University, London, and an MBA from London South Bank University. He is Senior Lecturer in Business Management at Middlesex University Business School, London. Dr Ekanem specializes in economic regeneration and small-business research, with particular focus on the financial management practices of small and medium-sized businesses, and has published his work in a number of reputable journals, including *The British Accounting Review, International Small Business Journal, Journal of Small Business and Enterprise Development, International Journal of Entrepreneurial Behavior and Research* and *International Journal of Consumer Studies*. He has written five book chapters and is a co-author of over 20 official reports. He is a fellow of the Higher Education Academy (FHEA).

Acknowledgements

The author of this book has developed the material over a lifetime, and many colleagues and friends have been constructive in this respect. The author would especially like to thank Dr Ian Vickers of the Centre for Enterprise and Economic Development research, Middlesex University, who has been a particularly helpful colleague in this respect.

1 Introduction to this book

Business planning is a very important part of a new business creation. There is a popular saying that 'if you fail to plan, you plan to fail'. This is a truism in entrepreneurship and new business development. Every venture requires diligent planning. If you are planning to start your own business, the first thing you need to do is to develop an effective business plan.

A business plan is a written document to describe a business opportunity, the goals of the business and the methods to achieve the goals. It is a road map for your business. A business plan fulfils two main objectives. The first objective of a business plan is that it serves as a strategic planning document for entrepreneurs (Deakins and Freel, 2012). In other words, it is a plan to guide the business and a basis for making strategic decisions, and it serves as a subsequent monitoring device. The second purpose of a business plan is to help you raise money from banks, investors or other lenders. It may also be required to obtain funding from agencies such as local enterprise agencies or local authorities. Many people pay more attention to the second function of a business plan than to the first. For all intents and purposes, the first is the most important.

As a road map, a business plan helps you to spell out exactly where your business is heading and how it intends to get there. To help you have a firm control of your business, it provides a fixed set of criteria against which you test every decision in the business. This means that a business plan is not a book to be left on the shelf to gather dust. It is a document you should keep on the table and work through continually, and it should be shared with everyone who is connected with the business.

Every business needs a clearly defined plan. As an entrepreneur, you will count on your business plan as a guide for your future business operations. When you develop the plan, you should keep in mind that you plan for the lifespan of your business. Without planning, you can make mistakes that will cost you large amounts of money.

Of course, there are some aspects of running your business that you can learn as you go along, but planning for your business is clearly not one of them. Oftentimes, there can be a great deal of complexity and difficulty involved in starting a business, but that does not have to be so. Proper planning will alleviate some of these challenges. It is important to note that starting a new business involves a wide range of activities for which you will need to make decisions straight away. You must also realize that there may be no time to establish what decision should be taken once you have opened the doors of your business. This is why you must plan in advance in order to avoid making expensive mistakes.

Ideh (2012: 21) emphasizes, 'You have no business without a plan.' I could not agree more with that statement. If you want your business to succeed and grow, you must have a plan. Without a clear plan of action, it is easy to lose direction of your business. A business plan will help you to plan your strategy, map your direction and stay on course.

If you want a business plan to have a great impact on your business, it must be genuinely related to your initial business idea. It would not be a great business plan if you simply fill in a template on the internet or even pay someone else to do it for you with no relationship whatsoever with your lofty business idea. It might look good, feel good, and give you that sense of satisfaction, but it would not do you any good without a good deal of input from you.

The business plan is an intricate part of the vision and purpose of the business. Therefore, it must be prepared and written by the original owner of business idea. It is not a document to be copied from the internet. It must be written in a way that reflects the vision of the business owner(s). The business owners must be prepared to adjust the plan as they go along the journey because, as a road map, the route may change as a result of road works or diversions.

As a senior lecturer and researcher with deep interest in entrepreneurship, economic regeneration, and small-business development, I have interviewed many small-business owners who have started their own businesses without a business plan. I have also come across many people who go into business with little or no knowledge or idea of the business that they have gone into. Some go into ventures for which they have no skills or experience. Consequently, they lose focus and direction of the business, and what seemed to be a great business idea in the beginning starts to dwindle and wither away simply because the start-up process was not well planned.

Therefore, before deciding to embark on a business venture, you need to carry out a 'self-analysis' which requires you to ask yourself serious questions such as the following:

- Who am I, and what do I want to achieve?
- Do I have the skills necessary to start a business, or should I first of all seek some kind of training?

- What kind of technical help do I need (i.e. accountants, lawyers, management consultants, computer specialists etc.)?
- Can I afford such assistance?
- What is the worth of the business opportunity?
- Can I relate the business opportunity to the market and industry conditions?
- Will I be able to sacrifice present benefits to concentrate on starting a business?
- Am I willing to take the risk to invest time, money and effort in the business?
- What do I expect from the business in the future?
- Where do I see myself in ten years' time?

It is only after answering these questions that you should develop a business plan.

The advantages of a business plan cannot be overemphasized. The first most important advantage of the document is that it helps the business owner to maintain a focus on the business strategy, competitive forces, risks and financial projections. The second most important advantage of a business plan is helping you to raise finance for the business. Therefore, the finance section of the business plan is very important.

Many entrepreneurs lack the financial skills to put this section together in a professional manner, and the lack of professionalism here can work against the enterprise on many levels. If a prospective investor cannot get a clear financial picture of the enterprise, it will certainly affect the chances of investing in the organization. This is another area where this book becomes handy as it seeks to show the reader how to go about it.

A major problem often encountered while designing a business plan is that different funding bodies may have different requirements. For example, while a bank manager may be interested in financial projections, the venture capitalist and business angel may require a more detailed business plan and more market analysis for the obvious reason that the venture capitalist or business angel may not be able to take a collateral security to safeguard their investment (Mason and Stark, 2004).

Similarly, an enterprise or development agency may vary in their requirements if a business plan is needed for funding (Deakins and Freel, 2012). Therefore, although the business plan is primarily written for management and strategic decision-making purposes, the business owner is advised to find out the format required by the funder. In this case, the entrepreneur should be prepared to adjust, modify, shorten or extend the plan to suit the requirements of the funder.

This book is written for academics, practitioners, entrepreneurs, would-be entrepreneurs and students. It is intended to be a practical 'how to do it' handbook which aims to ensure that readers have the knowledge and skills to develop a business plan, put it into operation, make decisions regarding their business and plan for growth and exit strategies. The book will remind the reader of appropriate basic academic theories and analytical tools to achieve a successful business start-up, grow the business and make important decisions on future strategies.

This book aims to facilitate the development of a unique business plan. A particular emphasis is placed on planning the business beyond the start-up phase. Especially important is the reconciliation of theory with practice. Finally, the book will help your business to get off not only to a cracking start but also to a growing stage!

In particular, the book will help readers to:

- explore business ideas and entrepreneurship, including feasibility, profitability, market analysis, competition and timing
- draft a business plan while choosing and shaping the best idea and growing their business beyond the start-up phase
- formalize the idea to enable the resourcing of the project, especially focusing on practicability, financing and market positioning
- be able to report to their investors using an investors' meeting and a company report.

On completion of this book, readers will be able to:

- master all the necessary business-function areas that need to be addressed in establishing and running a new venture
- identify and apply major strategies required by a management planning process for developing a new venture into the future
- define the day-to-day issues which confront a new and growing venture during its formative stages.

In summary, this book will enable readers to:

- produce a comprehensive and coherent business plan and critically evaluate the risks to its implementation
- implement all aspects of setting up, running and developing a new venture, including establishing a company, raising finance, marketing, staffing, premises, accounting records, production of final accounts, growth and exit strategies
- summarize progress of their company to date and present arguments for continued investment and growth to shareholders

- recognize the information needs of banks and equity investors
- present the achievements and aspirations of a new and growing venture to stakeholders effectively.

References

Deakins, D. and Freel, M. (2012) *Entrepreneurship and Small Firms*, sixth edition, McGraw-Hill, London.

Ideh, S. (2012) *Quick Win Tips for Entrepreneurs – Entrepreneurial Development Series*, Olad World of Creation Publishing, Nigeria.

Mason, C. and Stark, M. (2004) What do investors look for in a business plan? A comparison of the investment criteria of bankers, venture capitalists and venture capitalists. *International Small Business Journal*, 22, 227–248.

2   The contents of a business plan

It is impossible to be prescriptive in the content of a business plan since every business plan will be different and will be designed for different requirements. However, there are a number of standard sections that are normally included in a business plan. These sections are listed below and discussed in detail in subsequent chapters.

Cover sheet

The cover sheet should include:

- the name of the business
- the names of the directors
- addresses and telephone numbers of the business and directors.

Table of contents

This section should not be more than one page. The purpose of the table of contents is to help the reader to locate the section of interest easily.

Executive summary

The executive summary is the first major section of a business plan. However, it should be the last to be written since it is a summary of the main contents of the business plan. This section should state the purpose and objectives of the business plan. If the business owner's intention is to raise finance for the business, he/she should briefly state the legal structure of the business, where and when it was incorporated and why he/she needs to raise finance.

The executive summary should be a concise summary of your marketing, financial, operational and management/organizational plans. Ideally, a brief description of your markets and products/services will also be included in this section. It is important to bear in mind that some people will read only the executive summary. For this reason, the executive summary should capture the entire business plan.

Introduction

This is the first main section of your business plan and should provide information about the background of the business, such as a brief history of the business, how the business idea was conceived, the business name, business activities, the industrial sector, the unique selling point(s), the main aims and objectives of the business, and the legal form.

Business strategy

This section of the plan should discuss the vision and mission statements of the business. It should also discuss the strengths, weaknesses, opportunities and threats of the business. The location of the business as well as the names and addresses of the directors should be provided in this section of the plan.

Marketing research

In this section, you will report the results of your market research, both secondary and primary research analysis, comprising the market size, your target market, competitors, advertising and promotion techniques and selling strategy.

Finance

The finance section will cover the start-up costs, pricing strategy, daily cash collection, projected financial statements such as the cash flow statement, profit and loss account, the balance sheet and notes to the accounts. Financial ratios will also be presented in this section.

Operations management

The operations section will discuss the business premises and layout, equipment, sources of supply, the production process and customer service.

Human resources (HRM)

This section will provide information about the organization structure in the form of a chart, key people and functions, directors' profile, recruitment and training. Details of regulations affecting the business and its compliance will also be discussed in this section.

Risk analysis, growth and exit planning

This final section of the plan deals with all the hidden hazards which occupy the business owner's mind on a subconscious level but which should be carefully considered and documented on a conscious level in the business plan.

Conclusions

The concluding chapter gives a summary of the business plan and reiterates the main purpose of the plan. It summarizes the case for the business, why it will be successful, and how that has been demonstrated.

3 Introduction to the business plan

After the executive summary, this will be the first main chapter of your business plan. In this section, your first task is to identify your choice of business and to describe it vividly. If you are an existing entrepreneur, it is in this section that you will give a brief description of your business including the background of the business and how the business idea was arrived at. The description of your business and its activities is probably the most important part of your business plan.

If you have been in business for a while, you must give a brief history of your business. You must discuss your expertise and work experience and that of your partners, associates and managers. You must also explain the growth opportunities of your business and your reasons for believing your business will be successful.

If you are at a pre-start stage or considering setting up your business, you should be advised that your business idea must be such that it is capable of enthusing you as the business owner, your staff, customers and all other stakeholders. This enthusiasm must be reflected in the business plan. Your passion must be tangible in the business plan and must have a contagious effect on everyone else that comes in contact with it (Ideh, 2012). Therefore, it would be an error to go into a business in which you have no passion, interest, knowledge or skills. You cannot go into a business simply because your friend is in that line of business. Your business idea must be one that can get you out of your bed very early in the morning and keep you awake far into the middle of the night.

This section of the plan will describe the business activities and the industrial sector. It is also in this section of the plan that you will provide information about the name of your business and the legal form of ownership. There is no one 'best' form of ownership. The best decision depends on the entrepreneur's particular situation. The key to choosing a form of ownership is to understand how each firm's factors affect an entrepreneur's specific business and personal circumstances. Therefore, the legal form can be a sole trader, a partnership or a limited liability company.

The implication of the legal form to a sole trader or partnership is unlimited personal liability and limited access to capital. The disadvantages to a sole trader can also include limited skills and abilities and a feeling of isolation. As a limited liability company, the liability of the directors and potential shareholders is limited to the amount of capital that each of them has invested in the company. This form of incorporation will make the company more attractive to banks and other investors. The downside to this is the need to comply with more regulations and greater disclosure of information.

Summary

- The purpose of the business plan must be stated (e.g. Why is the plan being written? Who is it for? Do you want a loan, need more partners/shareholders, or need an agreed strategy among partners/directors?).
- You must also remember to state the reasons for choosing the business idea.
- A brief description of the business must be provided.
- The location of your business is important and should be disclosed in your business plan.
- It is also important to indicate the legal status of your business and why you have chosen that legal form for your business.

Reference

Ideh, S. (2012) *Quick Win Tips for Entrepreneurs – Entrepreneurial Development Series*, Olad World of Creation Publishing, Nigeria.

4 Idea generation

Idea generation is often influenced by the entrepreneur's past experience, training, education and skills. An idea can be generated and developed by the recognition that a particular product, service or process can be done better or in a superior way. The recognition that something can be done differently has impelled the development of many new businesses. Many new business ideas are oftentimes developed in the sectors or industries in which the would-be business owner has had previous experience. This demonstrates the importance of human capital as a determining factor in new business creation. Therefore, this chapter examines how new business ideas can be affected by creative thinking and opportunity recognition. The types of business ideas and the ingredients for success of new business ideas are also discussed.

Creative thinking

Creative thinking is very important in planning. For creative thinking to take place, the right environment and the right team of individuals are required. Creative thinking starts from recognizing that something (a product or service) 'could be done better' or from identifying a gap in the market (see Appendix 1). Creative thinking is the ability to connect previously unrelated things or ideas – i.e. lateral thinking rather than vertical thinking which defines a problem in one way only (Clegg, 1999).

Lateral thinking involves perceiving many possible divergent options rather than concentrating on a unique convergence. It also involves using imagination and being analytical rather than applying logic (Clegg, 1999). The right creative environment is important, and techniques (e.g. brainstorming to encourage the free flow of ideas; opportunity and problem mapping) can be used to help improve creative thinking.

Creative thinking can be influenced or shaped by discussion with the right team of individuals. It can also benefit from research, information gathering and feedback. Therefore, it should be pointed out that ideas rarely 'come out of the blue' – successful businesspeople spend time looking for opportunities and developing their ideas.

Opportunity recognition

Opportunity recognition is a key element of the business planning process. Opportunities can be created by change (whether political, economic, social, demographic or technological). For example, economic change can lead to a period of economic growth and increased demand for a set of products and services, which creates opportunities for new business ideas to take advantage of the increased affluence and spending power of the people (Rae, 2015).

Similarly, the increased pace of technological development has created opportunities for new business ventures such as computer software, web design and multimedia. The revolution in information and communication technology has resulted in a major growth of small-business applications in biotechnology.

Social and demographic change may provide business opportunities as a result of changing attitudes and ageing population structures. Changing attitudes may include changing attitude to failure. Recognition of a business idea calls for the right attitude towards risk and failure. You must be prepared to take a calculated risk. A calculated risk is a risk that has been given thoughtful consideration and for which the potential costs and benefits have been weighed and considered. Of course, the bigger the risk, the greater the reward! You must also be prepared to look at failure as a learning opportunity.

Different people from different cultures deal with failure differently. In the USA, failure is viewed as a learning experience, and people can benefit from it, learn from their experience and go on to form successful companies and other ventures as a result. In Britain, on the other hand, people are less tolerant of failure, and, too often, highly talented individuals have not been able to recover from it. A report by the Small Business Service indicates that as many as 40% of people in the UK would not start a business due to fear of failure, whereas the equivalent in the USA is 26%. However, this is now changing, and a change in cultural attitudes to risk and failure means that potential entrepreneurs can now recognize business opportunities more than before.

In opportunity recognition, there is need for correct timing. The market needs to be receptive and ready to accept the change (see Appendix 1).

Factors influencing the decision to start a new business idea

The first step to choosing your business is to be able to recognize an opportunity. An opportunity is defined as the potential for change, improvement or advantage arising from an action (Rae, 2007). Rae (2007) identifies four essential features of an opportunity:

- Demand – there must be a need, problem or potential demand to be satisfied. Demand is an economic principle that describes the desire and willingness of consumers to pay a price for a particular good or service. The greater the demand for your business idea/product or service, the greater the opportunity!
- Innovation – an idea for the product, service or experience to be provided must be innovative. It is important to point out here that the word 'innovation' does not necessarily mean a new invention. It means that the opportunity or business idea must have an added value, no matter how small the value added is. It is recognizing that a product or service 'could be done better' or identifying a gap in the market (see Appendix 1).
- Feasibility – the idea is feasible or doable with regard to the risks and complexities. This can be a hobby (see Appendix 2).
- Attractiveness – the idea or opportunity must have a potential reward and a level of interest to the entrepreneur. The rewards from an enterprise can be both financial and non-financial. The non-financial rewards can include a sense of satisfaction, building something, being one's own boss and in control, being an employer, getting an industry award or good publicity, or getting feedback from customers. Ultimately, it is the financial rewards that justify the effort and make taking the risk worthwhile.

Factors giving rise to opportunities can be divided into *pull factors* and *push factors*.

Pull factors

These are positive factors which influence or attract a person to start a business, which include:

- the desire to be independent
- the desire for greater job satisfaction
- turning a hobby or interest into something even more rewarding (see Appendix 2)

- spotting a gap in the market or exploiting an opportunity (see Appendix 1)
- making best use of experience and qualifications
- the desire to have flexibility
- finding an outlet for one's creativity
- the desire to make money or other financial incentives
- the desire to put something back in the society or community.

Push factors

These are negative factors associated with limited opportunities, which can force a person into self-employment. They include:

- unemployment or lack of employment opportunities
- redundancy
- job frustration
- limited or no promotion
- reaching the glass ceiling in present employment.

Types of start-up ideas

The development of new business ideas can consist of starting from scratch, buying a business as a going concern, buying as a franchise, or management buy-out and management buy-in.

Starting from scratch

An entrepreneur can decide to start a new business venture from the beginning. Starting a small business from scratch may have several advantages and disadvantages, depending on the new small-business venture. The advantages include high degree of autonomy, which means the ability to do as you like from the start. Starting a business from scratch may be cheaper as the business owner is able to avoid initial purchase costs. However, the disadvantage may include a potentially higher risk than other options. It may take time to build up the business and income, and there is no goodwill from customers or suppliers.

Buying a going concern

A business is said to be a going concern if the company has the resources needed to continue to operate indefinitely until a company provides evidence to the contrary. The term also refers to a company's ability to make enough money to stay afloat or avoid bankruptcy. An entrepreneur may decide to buy a business as a going concern rather than start from scratch. One of the advantages of such a business idea is that it might be less risky and there is customer and supplier goodwill.

Goodwill in accounting is an intangible asset that arises when a buyer acquires an existing business. It is the excess of the 'purchase consideration' (the money paid to purchase the asset or business) over the total value of the assets and liabilities. Another advantage of buying a business as a going concern is that funders are more ready to provide funding for the operation of the business as the business is in a position to provide immediate income.

However, buying a business as a going concern may require a high initial outlay. The purchaser may inherit problems such as poor staff. The goodwill may not last long as customers may decide to move on after the purchase.

Buying a franchise

The franchise is a type of a new business creation. The difference from other forms of business creation is that the franchisor, rather than the franchisee, undertakes much of the business creation process, including idea formulation and opportunity recognition. Franchising has grown in the last 20 years and is regulated by the British Franchise Association. Buying a franchise can have advantages as well as disadvantages. For example, a franchise provides an established product/service, know-how, marketing, a brand name, training and other supplies. It can benefit from economies of scale, e.g. in marketing, advertising and buying supplies. It can also be less risky; therefore, funders are more keen to lend. It is often favoured by banks due to an established track record.

However, a franchise may require large capital outlay from the franchisee. The trading area may be limited geographically; hence, growth of the business will be limited. There may be problems in the relationship between the franchisor and the franchisee, and there may also be financial disputes. Finally, strict agreements in terms of production, sales and marketing may limit innovation and growth.

Management buy-out/buy-in

Traditionally, management buy-outs (MBOs)/management buy-ins (MBIs) are not regarded as entrepreneurship or business creation. An MBO is the buy-out of the equity of a company by the existing manager or management team. An MBI involves an outside entrepreneur or team buying into the business. MBOs and MBIs are often funded by a venture capital institution. Both MBOs and MBIs may not be seen as creating new businesses. However, they often require pre-purchase planning and research and may result in the transformation of an old business – i.e. strategic re-orientation.

The ingredients for success of new business ideas

Planning is a continuous activity which interplays between planning and acting. The basic ingredients for the successful implementation of a business idea can be listed as follows:

- motivation and commitment – necessary drive
- ability and skill – technical, managerial, behavioural
- the idea in relation to the market – market need
- resources – sufficient premises, labour, materials, finance.

Other ingredients include:

- managing holistically – i.e. seeing the whole picture (e.g. set targets for all aspects of the business)
- communicating effectively to build up the customer base (e.g. build the brand through consistent and effective communication)
- building a fan club around the business by working effectively with people (e.g. carefully select employees and associates who can grow with the business)
- widening the talent pool and accessing and using expertise (e.g. develop a network of trusted advisors)
- managing business operations (e.g. identify what information will be produced on different aspects of the business)
- managing financial resources effectively (e.g. plan and control cash flow; ensure customers pay promptly).

Summary

A business idea takes time to formulate and research, and it may be considerably refined before the business is launched. Every business idea is unique, and the circumstances that contribute to success are intangible and may be different for each situation. The stages in the idea generation consist principally in creative thinking and opportunity recognition.

References

Clegg, B. (1999) *Creativity and Innovation for Managers*, Butterworth Heinemann, London.

Rae, D. (2007) *Entrepreneurship: From Opportunity to Action*, first edition, Palgrave Macmillan, London.

Rae, D. (2015) *Opportunity-Centred Entrepreneurship*, second edition, Palgrave Macmillan, London.

5 Business strategy

Having decided what type of business you are going to establish, you need to further explore, develop and refine your start-up idea. It is particularly important that you give sufficient consideration to the likely viability of the business idea. In this section of your business plan, you have to state your mission and vision. You also need to carry out analysis of the industry in which your business will be located, the business environment, and key success factors.

Mission statement

A mission statement is a sentence or a few sentences describing a company's function(s), markets and competitive advantage. It is a short statement of business goals and philosophies. A mission statement aims to represent your business, the customers you serve and the skills you intend to develop in order to fulfil your vision. The Mission statement is used to communicate to all the 'stakeholders', both inside and outside the company, what the company stands for and where it is heading. Issues addressed by the mission statement could include:

- the nature of the company's activities
- your customers and how you aim to serve them
- your values and beliefs
- your sources of competitive advantage or distinctiveness.

Note, however, that not all small businesses choose to adopt formal mission statements. The main thing is that you are clear about your aspirations and objectives for the business.

How is a mission statement created?

You can create a mission statement by writing down in one sentence what the purpose of your business is (see Appendix 6, for McDonald's mission statement as an example).

Vision statement

A vision statement also defines the organization's purpose, but it does so in terms of the organization's values rather than the bottom line measure. The organization's values are the guiding beliefs about how things should be done within the organization. A vision statement serves three functions. First, it communicates both the purpose and the values of the organization. Second, it gives employees direction about how they should behave. It inspires them to give their best. The third function of a vision statement is that it shapes customers' understanding of why they should patronize the organization.

A vision statement describes a firm's aspirations and 'what it really wants to be'. A vision statement should address the following questions:

- What would you like the future to be?
- What are the market opportunities?
- What are the skills and competencies needed to realize your vision?
- Are there any competencies that you need to improve on?

In creating your vision statement, you should also consider the following questions:

- Why are you in business?
- What do you want for your company and customers?
- Who are your customers?
- What image of your business do you want to convey to your customers, suppliers, employees and the public?
- What is the nature of your products and services?
- What factors determine pricing and quality? You must consider how these relate to the reasons for your business's existence.
- What level of service do you provide? Do your customers agree? You should not be vague here; you must define what makes your service so extraordinary.
- What roles do you and your employees play? Is there a good leadership style in your organization that organizes, challenges and recognizes employees?
- What kind of relationships will you maintain with suppliers? A good relationship with suppliers is one in which you are in partnership with them so that when you succeed, so do they.
- How do you differ from your competitors – better, cheaper or faster?
- How would you use technology, capital, processes, products and services to reach your goals?

How do you create a vision statement?

First and foremost, you will have to identify your organization's mission as defined above. Secondly, you uncover the real human value in that mission. Thirdly, you identify what you, your customers and stakeholders will value most about how to achieve the organization's mission. Fourthly, distil these values into the values the organization has or should have. Finally, combine your mission and values, and polish the words until you have a vision statement which is inspiring, energizing and motivating to everybody in the organization (see Appendix 7 for McDonald's vision statement as an example).

Objectives

In order to achieve your vision and mission, you will need to identify several key objectives. These objectives will most likely relate to the viability of the business, including longer-term survival and growth. What are your principal objectives both long term and short term? The short-term objectives are the objectives which your business seeks to achieve within the first three years of its operation, whilst the long term objectives are those that are achievable after the first three years. Examples of short-term objectives include increasing quarterly sales by 5% or cutting expenses by 3%. Long-term objectives might include opening a new store, expanding a new facility or increasing market share by 0.5%.

These objectives may be quantitative or qualitative. **Quantitative objectives** should be **SMART** – specific, measurable, achievable, relevant and timely. They should also be consistent with one another and communicable. **Qualitative objectives** are those objectives for the business which reflect other ideals/values you may have, for example with respect to:

- developing a culture which fosters learning and continuous improvement
- developing a culture which is honest
- providing responsive/superior customer service
- contributing to the local community
- minimizing the environmental impact of your business activity.

The ultimate goal of strategic planning is formulating goals and objectives, but you should bear in mind that nobody has ever formulated a perfect goal. However, formulating objectives should not be done by a trial-and-error process. You should formulate realistic, clearly stated goals and objectives. There is no reason to set goals that will never be achieved. This does not mean that you should not raise the stakes. Setting high goals and objectives will help you adjust your actions as well as challenge yourself and your employees to reaching them. Be reasonable on how and when the objectives will be achieved.

Be prepared to adjust your objectives at all times. To facilitate this process, you must complete contingency plans. These plans can be referred to as 'what-if' plans. By developing contingency plans, you avoid having to plan again from scratch. In fact, contingency plans are actually versions of your master plan adjusted for different scenarios.

Your industry

Easy of entry

The decision whether to start a particular type of business is partly dependent on the 'barriers to entry' or ease of entry and the level of existing competition and response of existing firms. For many small start-ups, such considerations are likely to vary considerably according to where you decide to be located (see key points on locational considerations in the next chapter).

There are several barriers to entry, including the following: access to distribution channels; brand preferences and customer loyalty; capital requirements; economies of scale; cost advantages independent of size; inability to gain access to technology, specialized knowledge, raw materials, locations etc.; regulatory policies; tariffs; and international trade restrictions.

In carrying out industry analysis, you will have to ask yourself the following questions: *How easy is it to start up in your chosen area of business? What are the barriers to entry in your industry? Will you be able to overcome these? If not, you may need to re-think your start-up idea.*

Competition

A competitor is any organization that pursues the same group of customers or tries to satisfy the same set of customer needs. Before you can gain a competitive advantage, you need to know who your current competitors are and who your potential competitors are. You will need to carry out a competitors' analysis in order to identify what their relative strengths are. It is also important to identify the strategies they have adopted to establish their market position. This analysis will help you to identify any advantage they may have over you. Competitive advantages may arise out of relationships, reputation or innovation.

Relationships are developed with customers, suppliers, employees, investors, governments and competitors. Such relationships can be subdivided into internal relationships (employees), external relationships (customers, suppliers, investors, governments and competitors) and networks (groups of businesses engaged in related activities).

What will be the key relationships for your business?

Reputation and word-of-mouth recommendation can be particularly important for small businesses. It is the market's method for dealing with the attributes of quality which people cannot easily monitor themselves. If customers, for instance, cannot determine product quality by search or experience, they will be influenced by reputation. Reputation can be hard to gain but easy to lose, and so constant vigilance and attention to quality and customer needs is essential.

How will you promote the reputation of your business?

Innovation, particularly technical innovation, can be costly, uncertain and hard to manage – and the rewards are difficult to keep. Innovation can provide a competitive advantage, but it is dependent on management and other distinctive capabilities or strategic assets which can determine its future.

How relevant is innovation to your business, and what type of innovation is it?

Unique selling points

This is the section in which you flag up your competitive advantages. The ability to convey clearly what makes your business unique and attractive is very important as it highlights what will make the business successful. For instance, are you able to offer anything that your competitors do not? Your unique selling points could consist of the following:

- Niche market – can you point to a niche in the market that you are exploiting?
- Value added – the addition of features to a basic line or model for which the buyer is prepared to pay extra; additional features which go beyond the standard expectations and provide something more (see further as discussed below).

Will your product/service have any unique selling points (USPs)?

The key success factors

Your unique selling points can be your key success factors. Key success factors determine the financial and competitive success in the industry. Firms can win competitive advantage in an industry by concentrating on one or two key success factors, e.g.:

- **skills related** – design, information technology etc.
- **organization capability** – information systems, response times, management etc.
- **distribution related** – low cost, fast delivery, network etc.
- **marketing related** – sales force, packaging, service etc.
- **technology related** – research, innovatory, process etc.
- **manufacturing related** – low cost, efficiency, high utilization etc.
- **other factors** – such as reputation, location, layout, patents, collection of money, terms of business etc.

Where else can you add value?

Value can be added in four areas – product; service; delivery/point of sale; and price:

- **Product** – you can add value by distinguishing a product from others, to make it more attractive to customers through the company's capability, functional features or design, engineering features, quality, reliability, value etc.
- **Service** – value can be added through after-sales services, assistance provided, delivery, employees, pick up, policies etc.
- **Delivery** – you can add value with point-of-sale delivery, accessibility, convenience, location etc.
- **Price** – value can be added through unique benefits at a high price or equivalent benefits at a low price.

Oftentimes, managers focus only on the product and price areas, while ignoring the other two. It would be a mistake to do so.

Analyzing your business environment

You may find it useful to develop a SWOT or PEST analysis. A SWOT analysis involves the identification of strengths, weaknesses, opportunities and threats for the business. This usually consists of a series of bullet points under each heading, which should also match well with the content of the rest of the business plan. Although the SWOT analysis is subject to personal preference and views, it is best to be honest and avoid having a long list of strengths and only a short list of weaknesses, which is more likely to raise suspicions about the realism of the plan rather than impress.

A PEST analysis seeks to describe the degree to which the business environment is affected by key political, economic, social and technological factors:

- **Political** factors include employment and environmental protection legislation; foreign trade regulations; health and safety regulations; monopoly legislation; and taxation.
- **Economic** factors consist of business cycles; disposable income; prices; productivity; unemployment; and wage rates. Regional variations and trends are important.
- **Sociological** factors comprise attitudes to work and leisure; income distribution; levels of education; lifestyle changes; population demographics; social mobility and values; and ecological issues.
- **Technological** factors may include new discoveries/developments which may have particular relevance; rates of technical obsolescence; speed of technology transfer; consumer/user attitudes to new products etc.

In analyzing the environment, you will need to also answer the following questions:

- What is the nature and rate of change of the environment?
- What do you base your forecasts of the future on?
- How do you foresee your organization evolving in response to change? You will have to describe the degree to which the environment is likely to confront your organization with new situations.

Summary

- Vision/mission statement – remember to include a short mission statement in your business plan to describe your company goals and philosophies. A short vision statement should also be included in your business plan to describe the organization's value and beliefs about how things are done within the organization.
- Short-term/long-term objectives – your objectives should be specific, measurable, achievable, relevant and timely.
- Market context/business environment: e.g. SWOT or PEST (depending on the purpose of the business plan, one of these done thoroughly should be sufficient). These should analyze how easy it is to start up in your chosen area of business; what the barriers to entry are in your industry; and whether you will be able to overcome the barriers.
- USP/market niche/focus – your unique selling points could be a niche in the market which you are exploiting or could be value added.

6   Market research and marketing

The market research you conduct will be crucial in terms of providing an evidence base for the viability of your business, particularly in terms of identifying the extent to which there is likely to be demand for your product/service, refining your understanding of customer needs, and underpinning your marketing strategy.

There are two broad types of research to consider: primary and secondary. Secondary research involves collecting and reviewing existing sources of data relevant to your business/industry (e.g. industry journals, organization websites, academic sources, national statistics etc.).

Primary research will involve you in collecting your own data, e.g. through a small survey, key informant interviews (e.g. with a few industry experts, or somebody who runs a similar business) and/or perhaps a focus group of potential customers. Business owners are often busy and difficult to gain access to, so do take advantage of any existing contacts you may have, such as family or friends who are involved in small business. If you do approach outside organizations/businesses, be sure that you are clear about what you need, and do not waste their time. Note that focus groups can be particularly difficult to set up, but, if appropriate, you could ask a few friends and/or family members to participate in such a group.

Define your research objectives as carefully as possible. Exactly what do you want to know? Who should you sample for this information? In what ways can you best present your data and conclusions? Where are you going to collect the information, and when? Be realistic about what you can achieve with limited time and resources. Write a set of questions you think you will need to ask potential customers – this will form the basis for your questionnaire. Try out these questions before you do the field research and modify them until you are happy with them.

In this chapter, you have to introduce the marketing strategy you will use to enter the market and gain your market share. Your marketing plan should illustrate how you will market your products/services to make a profit. It is important to carefully define your target market and analyze its size and nature, while explaining why you chose the market. You must also describe your potential customers, how you plan to attract and retain them, and their financial profiles, needs, purchasing behaviour, price sensitivity etc.

In addition to the competition analysis carried out in the previous chapter, you need to assess your direct and indirect competition, comparing their business practices to your own. You must analyze the number of competitive firms and their locations, distribution channels, suppliers, pricing strategies and competitive advantages.

You must also outline sales promotion plans, advertising programmes, selling methods, purchasing plans, suppliers, distributors, and research and development. To make it easy for you, these points have been summarized below in bullet-point format.

Some guidelines for questionnaire design

- Keep the number of questions to a minimum.
- Have a cut-out question at the beginning to eliminate unsuitable respondents.
- Make sure you have an identifying question to show the cross-section of respondents.
- Keep the questions simple and unambiguous.
- Avoid biased or leading questions.
- Answers to survey questions should be Yes/No/Don't Know, or offer at least four alternatives.
- You may also want to include a few more open questions, particularly where you need a more exploratory approach and/or where you are seeking more in-depth insight from a small number of selected interviewees.
- Is there a market for your product or service, and can you get sufficient market share to support the business?

At least twelve areas need to be considered

- Who are your customers?
- What do they have in common?
- What are their needs?
- Where are they?
- In what ways can you sell to them?
- In what ways can you get the product/service to them?
- What is the state of the market – expanding, contracting, static?

- What social, economic, technological, legal, political factors etc. affect the market?
- What competition exists?
- What are your strengths and weaknesses, and what are those of the competition?
- What size of market share can be gained?
- What are the required terms of trade?

Analyze the market

What is the nature, extent and potential of your market?

- What is the size of the local market?
- What is the size of the national market (if you will be trading nationally)?
- What is the size of the international market (if you will be trading internationally)?
- What seasonal or periodic changes significantly affect the market (if any)?
- Is the market likely to expand, contract or remain the same size in the foreseeable future?
- If it is going to change, estimate the percentage of expansion or contraction per year. Is the market generally volatile or stable?
- Are there any other relevant comments that could be made on the market (e.g. changes in legislation; technology; other social, economic, or environmental aspects affecting the business)?
- Where did you get information about the market? Is it reliable?

Social status/occupational groups for identifying customers

These can be presented in a table as below:

Table 6.1 Social Status/Occupational Groups

A	Upper middle	Top managerial, administrative and professional
B	Middle	Intermediate managerial, administrative and professional
C1	Lower middle	Supervisory clerical, junior managerial
C2	Skilled working class	Skilled manual workers
D	Working class	Semi-skilled and unskilled manual workers
E	Lowest levels of subsistence	Widows, state pensioners, casual labour

Some other ways in which customers can be classified are:

- age
- gender
- profession/occupation
- educational level
- skills
- self-employed
- event specific – e.g. people getting married etc.
- geographically
- culture
- language
- beliefs – e.g. religious, political
- ownership groups – e.g. pets, cars, houses
- habits/tastes
- interest groups – e.g. hobbies, clubs, sports etc.
- business size – e.g. employing more than 20 people; turnover of less than £1m
- industry specific – e.g. oil industry, domestic, commercial, wholesale, retail
- type specific – e.g. independent plumbers, co-operatives, disabled
- weight, height, size
- marital status
- technology specific
- parental status
- ethnic group
- financial

Identify customer needs/benefits, such as:

- product or service suitable for customer's purpose (right product, right quality)
- confidence in your expertise/status
- after-sales service or support
- pleasant service or environment
- honesty, fulfilment or satisfaction
- flexibility
- competitive price, delivery, reliability, other terms of trade

Consider the following points when collecting, analyzing and presenting information about your customers:

- Who will be, or who are, your main groups of customers (e.g. type of individual, type of organization, etc.)?
- What is the customer looking for in the product/service (including price issues)?

- How far does your product/service go to meeting these requirements?
- What are the best ways of selling your product/service to the customer?
- Are there any other relevant comments you could make on your customers?

In addition to your competition strategy in Chapter 5 above, analyze your competitors and your relationship with them

- What gives you an advantage over your competitors?
- What advantages do your competitors have over you?
- What other relevant factors are there about your competitors?
- Does your product/service have a 'unique selling point'? If so, what is it?

Promotional tools

The following are the main types of promotional tools you may use. You may not use all of these, but select those that are beneficial to you in your type of business.

- Advertising – place an advert in a suitable media, either advertising the product as available (if it is) or offering further information to people who respond.
- Mail shots – send details to a sample of potential customers. If, for example, 5 in 100 will buy from you, you have gained valuable information and have started to develop a marketing strategy.
- Leaflet distribution – sample a target group or area, and gauge the response.
- Demonstration – arrange to give demonstrations of your product/ service, and use these to gauge the level of interest.
- Small-scale trading – purchase or manufacture a small number for sale to 'see how they go' – e.g. a retailer might place a small order for a new product and/or work on a basis of 'sale or return'.
- Sale by samples – samples only are made and shown or exhibited to potential customers. Responses are gauged. Provision can be made against firm orders.
- Trade exhibitions – these can be a useful way to make contact with potential customers and gauge their interest and also to see what the competitors are doing.

Marketing mix

A mix of ingredients can produce different end results. For example, a high-quality image with a prestige location and sophisticated advertising is not consistent with very low prices and untidy staff. Aspects of the 'marketing mix' to consider are:

- product – design, quality, after-sales service etc.
- production – i.e. in relation to the production capabilities of the business
- pricing policy
- promotion – advertising etc.
- people – service advice, support relationships etc.
- place – i.e. the location of the business and outlets

Note that some of these elements interrelate closely with the 'operations' aspects of the business (see Chapter 8).

Customer service

What do your customers expect from:

- the business?
- the staff?
- the products, goods or services?

Are you going to have a customer care policy? How will you implement it?

Advertising and promotion

- What do you want to happen?
- How much expenditure is appropriate and affordable?
- What messages do you want to project?
- What media should be used?

Locational considerations

- Proximity to customers and accessibility
- Proximity to competitors
- Availability/cost of suitable premises
- Backup services and supplies
- Infrastructure – roads, parking, public transport
- Is location conducive to image?
- Area of low or high growth?

Summary

- Nature of market – in terms of size (local, national and international markets as applicable); seasonal fluctuations; legislative, technological, social, economic or environmental changes affecting the market
- Competitor analysis – in terms of number of competitors and their locations, distribution channels, suppliers, pricing strategies and competitive advantages
- Customers – findings from desk research, surveys, focus groups etc. This should show social status, age, gender, common need etc.
- Promotion/advertising – indicate whether word of mouth, mailshots, leafleting, exhibitions etc.
- Sales/pricing – including competitive price, after-sales service/support etc.

7   Financing the business

The finance section is probably the most difficult part of the business plan to prepare for most business owners. Therefore, the author has focused more on this chapter in order to throw more light onto the process.

Apart from serving as a strategic planning document, the business plan will help you to raise finance for your business. This is money and other assets you will need in starting and running your business. Therefore, there are two most crucial questions you must ask yourself at this stage:

- What are my business's realistic financial needs? In other words, what capital do I need to launch my business?
- How do I satisfy these needs?

Usually, a combination of various sources is used to finance a business. Basically, there are two categories of financing: debt financing and equity financing.

Debt financing

This is money borrowed (usually from a bank to get the business started) which will have to be repaid eventually. Whilst you are making use of the money, you will have to pay interest on the loan. As far as debt finance is concerned, banks may be the first port of call and probably the only financial institution for most start-ups. The thing to remember about banks is that they are not in the risk business (Burns, 2014). They are looking to obtain a certain rate of interest over a specified period of time and to see their capital repaid. They do not share in the extra profits a business might make, so they do not expect to lose money if the firm encounters any problem. In addition, the bank manager stands to lose a lot if he or she lends to a business that subsequently fails. Therefore, your business plan should demonstrate clearly how the interest on the loan will be paid even in the worst possible set of circumstances and how the capital will be repaid on the due date. In this respect, the bank manager will be particularly interested in the cash flow forecast for at least two years (three years in some cases). Your business plan should demonstrate the cash-generating potential of the business for the three-year period. The bank manager will also be particularly interested in the breakeven and other key financial ratios such as gearing ratios, which must ideally be as low as possible.

Equity financing

This is money put into the business by the owner or shareholders through an initial public offering (IPO) if it is a public company. Shareholders may withdraw their money, and they expect the directors to increase the value of their shares and provide a stream of dividends. If you do not meet shareholders' expectations, they may sell their shares or refuse to provide more money, and they may change the board. Through an IPO, you may sell shares of your company to the public. However, this is usually the last resort used to raise finance for small businesses. Investors often consider this form of investment to be risky.

Equity finance for small businesses or start-ups is usually mainly through personal investment by the founder or family. This is the most common source of finance for small firms because of the essential conservatism of many business owners towards both debt and external equity. It is also because of the difficulty which some firms face in raising external finance such as the lack of collateral security, a good business plan, a track record etc.

Equity finance can also be in the form of money left in the business by way of retained profit. It is important to mention here that if the business is a completely new venture or a start-up, there will not be any retained profit to use at this stage.

In addition to making use of personal savings or borrowing from friends and family, associates, shareholders, or retained profits, equity finance can also be raised from venture capitalists or business angels. A venture capital can be defined as a financial investment in unquoted companies, which have significant growth potential, with a view to yielding substantial capital gains in line with the additional risk (Deakin and Freel, 2012). Therefore, it is capital that clearly involves a degree of risk. A business angel is informal risk capital or private individuals who invest smaller sums than venture capitalists in small companies. They are direct private equity rather than established financial institutions.

If these investors decide to invest in your company, they will offer their capital in exchange for an ownership stake in your company. Undoubtedly, this will put pressure on your business. In a way, these investors will attempt to 'control' your business and 'force' it to become profitable in the very first years of operation.

Prospective equity investors will normally expect to see a business plan before making up their minds whether or not to invest in your company. Therefore, their decision whether to proceed beyond reading your business plan depends on the quality of your plan. The quality of your business plan should be captured in the executive summary as most investors read only the executive summary. A business plan intended to be presented to equity investors should be longer, better presented, more comprehensive and offering greater detail. This is because equity investors share in both the risk and the return from the business. Because of this, they need to be convinced that both the entrepreneur and their team are as good as the business idea.

Financing requirements

In addition to the two fundamental questions above, you will also need to ask yourself the following questions:

- Why do you need the money?
- What type of money do you need?
- When will you need it?
- What deal are you offering your investors?
- What exit routes are open to your investors?

Loan criteria – the five Cs

Bank managers assess loan applications from small firms in terms of the following:

- Character – can the bank trust you? This may consist of the owner-managers' characteristics such as qualifications and experience in the field of business.
- Capacity – financial strength and past record. In other words, the bank manager will consider the viability of the business proposition or business case made in the business plan.
- Capital – you must be prepared to sink your own money in the business. The bank manager will definitely consider the extent of the client's stake in the business. The more capital you put into the business, the better your chances of getting the loan!
- Collateral – banks are not risk takers. Therefore, they need a collateral security in the form of a building property.
- Conditions – the bank will consider the prevailing economic, industry and local conditions.

Factors that affect credit scoring include your credit history, debt/equity ratio and working capital. The monthly debt repayment must be less than 40% of the monthly income.

What balance of debt to equity is 'right'?

Debt has to be serviced irrespective of your business performance. Therefore, it follows that in a risky, volatile marketplace, you stand a good chance of being caught short of money. If your risks are low, the chances are that profits will be low too. This is because high profits and low risks always attract a flood of competitors. This reduces prices and so reduces profits to a level which then represents the riskiness of the business. Therefore, a 1:1 gearing ratio would be ideal.

What do financiers look for?

Sources of debt capital like banks are looking for asset security to back their loan in order to be sure of getting their money back on demand. They also charge an interest rate which reflects the current market conditions and their view of the risk level of the current proposal. Therefore, bankers are interested in a steady stream of earnings in order to pay the interest rate rather than interested in growth in the value of the business over the long term.

Venture capitalists will not be interested in low-risk, low-return businesses, since they are looking for much better returns than investing in a portfolio of shares on the stock market. They will expect a return on their investment of about 40% with a view to an exit in 3–5 years plus a non-executive seat on the board and a share of the equity.

A good business plan often has clearly defined milestones. Each stage will incur major costs, and so the business should be worth more at the end of the stage. It is at these points that you can raise extra finance.

Sources of debt and equity

The sources of debt and equity can be tabulated as in Table 7.1:

Table 7.1 Sources of Debt and Equity

Debt Capital	Shareholder Funds
Banks – overdrafts	Private investors
– term loans	Venture capital
Government loans	Going public
Factoring	Industry
Leasing	Franchising
Finance Houses	

Making forecasts

Although the whole business plan is based on forecasts, the finance chapter is based more on forecasts and projections. Forecasting is not just randomly guessing about the future. Rather, it is an important tool that helps you correctly plan for your business. Although forecasting could be complicated, it is important to understand the substance of forecasts and to apply them appropriately to your planning process. As a business owner, you are in the best position to understand these forecasts as they apply to your business. For example, an economic downturn might hurt your business, especially if your product is expensive. Understanding this type of forecast will not reduce the risk to your business at start up, but it will help you forecast sales more accurately.

It is important to ensure that your forecasts or projections are reasonable. You are not making them 'conservative' by only stating that your projections are conservative. Make sure that you do not rush into projecting a moderate growth rate in sales in the first year, only to be followed by a sharp increase in sales in the second or third year. Ensure that your growth-rate assumptions are consistent and credible. Do not try to 'fool' bankers and investors with your assumptions. Remember that they have seen hundreds, maybe thousands, of business plans.

The sales forecast

While forecasts may be wrong, it is important to demonstrate in your business plan that you have thought through the factors that will have an impact on performance. You must show how you can deliver satisfactory results even when many of the factors are against you. Remember there is a difference between maximum capacity and optimum capacity. Optimum capacity is producing a great number of goods or services with minimum cost, while maximum capacity is the highest or greatest amount that can be received or contained, connoting volume.

You need to determine the unit cost for your products or services. You must decide how many units you will need to sell to cover your costs. You may not do this from the first month of trading. Initially you may even be working at a loss. You must assume a steady growth in sales over the months to come, say 10% per month (allowing, if necessary, for seasonal variations). You must also determine your break-even point.

Bankers measure the risks by evaluating the worst scenario and its likely effects, and they also look for an ultimate exit route. Therefore:

- Your sales forecasts must be believable.
- How much do you need to earn to pay your way?

- Provide details of all customers to whom you expect to sell.
- Provide the supporting market research data.
- Support your forecast with examples from other ventures.

Start-up costs

You need to show in detail how you plan to spend the money raised to start your business. In this respect, you need to create a capital equipment list that includes all equipment, machinery, fixtures and fittings needed by the business. This list may help you obtain the loan; sometimes, the capital equipment can serve as collateral. Your start-up costs will include those on the list in Table 7.2:

Table 7.2 Start-Up Costs and Expenditure

• Equipment	X
• Machineries	X
• Fixtures and fittings	X
It will include variable costs such as:	
• Materials etc. required to start the business	X
It will also include regular outgoings such as:	
• Rent	X
• Rates	X
• Electricity	X
• Gas	X
• Telephone	X
• Wages etc.	X
Total	X

The financial statements

Financial statements are a formal record of the financial activities of a company. They are written reports that quantify the financial strength, performance and liquidity of a company. There are three most important types of financial statements of a company, namely, the cash flow forecast, the balance sheet, and the profit and loss account.

These statements are required for at least three years and must be supported by the various performance ratios over the years of the business plan. Identify the assumptions underpinning your forecasts. Work out your financial performance ratios.

(1)   Cash flow forecast

Remember that profit is not cash and that cash is not profit. Therefore, a cash flow statement is not the same as a profit and loss account. A business can survive in the short term if it is not making a profit so long as it has sufficient cash reserves. It cannot survive without cash even though it may be making a profit. The cash flow forecast shows how much cash is required to reach the objectives of the business and when it will be needed. Forecasts are required for at least three years (some funders may require up to five years of forecasts).

New and fast-growing businesses need more cash than you would expect since they may not be making enough profits from the beginning in order to finance the current business or its expansion. This is because there is a delay which needs financing between buying the materials and collecting the money from the sold goods.

Therefore, a cash flow forecast shows the projected income from sales and other sources and all the expenses around the launch and operation of the business. In other words, a cash flow statement is an analysis of all changes that affect cash during a period of time. It shows both sources of cash (e.g. cash from a loan, the entrepreneur's personal savings or sales) and uses of cash (e.g. acquisitions of equipment, payments of salaries/wages, insurance, taxes, utilities, raw materials etc.). In other words, it shows both the income and the expenditure of the business. There is a need to show the timing of income and expenses for 12 monthly periods over a minimum period of three years. It is important to remember to make it clear what assumptions underlie your projections – e.g. sales increase per month, date when loan repayments begin, extra workers taken on etc. Table 7.3 below is an example of a cash flow forecast.

Example

Suppose you are planning to start your business (B. Smart Ltd) by injecting £100,000 as capital – half of it at the start of the business in January and the other half in June. You also plan to make £10,000 every month in sales in the business. You expect income from sales of property of £8,500 on January and another £8,500 in June.

B. Smart Ltd is also expected to incur the following expenses:

- Plant and equipment of £130,000 is to be purchased and paid for in two instalments: one at the start of the business in January and one in June.
- Purchases of £65,000 for the accounting year are to be made, spread equally over the 12-month period.
- An annual rent of £10,000 is expected to be paid in equal monthly instalments.
- Salaries of £1,500 are to be paid every month.
- Lighting and heating of £4,000 per annum is to be paid quarterly.
- Income tax of £12,000 is to be paid in December.

From the above information, your cash flow statement can be presented as follows:

Table 7.3 B. Smart Ltd Cash Flow Statement for the Year …

Receipts	Jan	Feb	Mar	Apr	May	Jun	Jul	Aug	Sep	Oct	Nov	Dec	Total
	£	£	£	£	£	£	£	£	£	£	£	£	£
Sales	10,000	10,000	10,000	10,000	10,000	10,000	10,000	10,000	10,000	10,000	10,000	10,000	120,000
Capital	50,000					50,000							100,000
Sale of Property	8,500					8,500							17,000
Total Receipts (A)	68,500	10,000	10,000	10,000	10,000	68,500	10,000	10,000	10,000	10,000	10,000	10,000	237,000
Payments													
Plant and Equipment	65,000					65,000							130,000
Purchases	5,416	5,416	5,416	5,416	5,417	5,417	5,417	5,417	5,417	5,417	5,417	5,417	65,000
Rent	833	833	833	833	833	833	833	833	833	833	833	837	10,000
Salaries	1,500	1,500	1,500	1,500	1,500	1,500	1,500	1,500	1,500	1,500	1,500	1,500	18,000
Lighting and Heating	–	–	1,000	–	–	1,000	–	–	1,000	–	–	1,000	4,000
Income tax	–	–	–	–	–	–	–	–	–	–	–	12,000	12,000
Total Payments (B)	72,749	7,749	8,749	7,749	7,750	73,750	7,750	7,750	8,750	7,750	7,750	20,754	239,000
Net Cash Flow (A–B)	(4,249)	2,251	1,251	2,251	2,250	(5,250)	2,250	2,250	1,250	2,250	2,250	(10,754)	(2,000)
Opening Balance	0	(4,249)	(1,998)	(747)	1,504	3,754	(1,496)	754	3,004	4,254	6,504	8,754	
Closing Balance	(4,249)	(1,998)	(747)	1,504	3,754	(1,496)	754	3,004	4,254	6,504	8,754	(2,000)	

A cash flow statement is useful in three areas. First, it helps you to plan how much sales you are expecting in a particular year. Second, it helps you to plan how much expenditure you expect to make. Third, it helps you to understand when cash is likely to come into, and leave, your business, thus revealing the critical months that you should be particularly careful about. In the example above, the months of January, June and particularly December are critical months for B. Smart Ltd.

Therefore, a cash flow forecast will help you make important decisions regarding whether and when you can afford to recruit new staff, rent more office accommodation, borrow more money, or take more money out of the business and will help you determine when you might be at risk of running out of cash.

(2)   *Balance sheet*

A balance sheet is a financial statement which shows the financial position of a business at a particular point in time. In other words, it is a snapshot picture of assets and liabilities at any particular time, after 12 months of trading. The most important assumption to remember when preparing your balance sheet is to state the depreciation rate used.

A balance sheet is normally comprised of the following three elements:

- **Assets** – these are things owned by a company such as a plant and machinery (which are often referred to as fixed assets) and cash and stock in trade (which are often referred to as currents assets).
- **Liabilities** – liabilities are things which a company owes to someone else or another company (e.g. creditors, bank loans etc.).
- **Equity** – this is what the company owes to its owners such as the amount of capital that remains in the company after using its assets to pay off its liabilities. Therefore, equity is the difference between the company's assets and its liabilities.

It is important to point out that the total assets of a company must be equal to the sum of the liabilities. This is because the total assets of a business must be equal to the amount of capital invested by the owners (i.e. in the form of share capital and retained profits) and any borrowings.

Example

The following is an illustrative example of a simple balance sheet. Suppose you invest £130,000 in a plant and equipment in your business (B. Smart Ltd) and £37,000 in stocks, of which you have sold £25,000 worth of goods on credit. Your cash at bank or in hand stands at £8,000, and your current liabilities are trade creditors (£35,000) and bank overdrafts (£10,000). Apart from the trade creditors and bank overdrafts, your assets in the business are financed from internal sources such as share capital of £100,000 and retained earnings of £15,000. Your balance sheet would appear as follows:

Table 7.4 B. Smart Ltd Balance Sheet as at . . .

Fixed Assets	£	£
Plant and Equipment		130,000
Current Assets		
Stocks	12,000	
Debtors	25,000	
Cash	*8,000*	*45,000*
		175,000
Less Current Liabilities		
Trade Creditors	35,000	
Bank Overdrafts	*10,000*	*(45,000)*
Net Worth		*130,000*
Financed By		
Share Capital	100,000	
Reserves	2,000	
Retained Earnings	*28,000*	*130,000*

The balance sheet enables financial analysts to assess the financial health of a business. If balance sheets are analyzed over two or three accounting periods, they are useful in identifying underlying trends in the financial position of the business such as the business's liquidity and other business-related risks. When analyzed in combination with other financial statements of the business and those of its competitors, a balance sheet may assist in identifying relationships and trends which are indicative of potential problems or areas for further improvement. A proper analysis of the balance sheet of a company can assist the user to predict how the company is likely to perform in the future.

(3)   *Profit and loss account*

In addition to the balance sheet, a projected income statement for at least the first three years of operation should be developed. This income statement is often referred to as a profit and loss account. A profit and loss account is a moving picture of how well the business is doing in terms of sales, costs, and profitability, it is usually prepared to cover an accounting period of one year. It involves adding up all trading income and subtracting the costs of goods sold to get the gross profit or loss. The net profit is arrived at by subtracting total general expenses for the year (including depreciation) from the trading profit.

The profit and loss statement is prepared on the accrual basis of accounting. This means that all revenues are recognized when they are **earned** rather than when receipts are realized (although in many cases income may be earned and received in the same accounting year). Conversely, expenses are recognized in the profit and loss account when they are **incurred** even if they are paid for before or after the accounting period. A profit and loss account consists of the following main components:

Sales or turnover – this includes income or revenue earned from the principal activities of the business. For example, if you manufacture hand towels, your sales, turnover or revenue will consist of the sales from the hand towels. Conversely, if you earn interest on your other investments or gain on disposal of fixed assets, such interests or gains will be regarded not as sales or revenue but as 'other income'.

Cost of sales – this represents the cost of goods sold or services rendered during an accounting period. For a retailer, the cost of sales is essentially the opening stock plus purchases during the accounting year minus any closing stock. However, for a manufacturer, the cost of sales is the product costs incurred in the manufacture of goods during an accounting period. Such costs will include direct labour, direct material, depreciation of plant and machinery and factory overheads, etc.

Expenses – these are the overheads incurred with regard to the accounting period irrespective of whether they were paid in the previous accounting period or in a subsequent accounting period. These include rents, salaries, lighting and heating, telephone, insurance, professional fees, administrative expenses, finance charges etc.

Example

Suppose at the end the accounting period the Trial Balance of your company, B. Smart Ltd, shows the following information:

Table 7.5 Trial Balance of B. Smart Ltd

	Dr	Cr
	£	£
Sales		120,000
Purchases	77,000	
Other Income		17,000
Rent	10,000	
Salaries	18,000	
Lighting and Heating	4,000	

As you can see, these figures are also contained in your cash flow statement above. Your trading profit and loss account would be as presented in Table 7.6 below.

Table 7.6 B. Smart Ltd Trading and Profit and Loss Account
for the Year Ended . . .

	£	£
Sales		120,000
Purchases	77,000	
Less Stock	(12,000)	
Cost of Goods Sold		*65,000*
Gross Profit		55,000
Other Income		17,000
Less Expenses		
Rent	10,000	
Salaries	18,000	
Lighting and Heating	*4,000*	*(32,000)*
Profit before Tax		40,000
Income Tax		*(12,000)*
Net Profit		*28,000*

A profit and loss (or income) statement provides the basis for measuring performance of a business over an accounting period. The performance can be measured in terms of change in sales revenue over the period and in comparison to industry growth; change in gross profit margin and net profit margin over the period; and comparison of the company's profitability with other companies operating in similar sectors or industries.

Sensitivity analysis

You will also need to carry out a sensitivity analysis of how susceptible your business will be to changes and as a test of the robustness of the business to unforeseen changes and note how much each of the following have to change to affect the viability of the Plan. This is usually done only for the first year of operation – e.g. what happens if:

* *Optimistic scenario*

    Sales and other income are increased by 10% – you will need to adjust expenses to allow for this, including for increased costs of materials etc. and possibly salary costs.

• *Pessimistic scenario*

Sales and other income decrease by 10% – you will equally need to adjust to allow for this change.

Break-even analysis

Break-even analysis is a key component of a good business plan. Break-even, in simple terms, refers to the point where all costs (fixed and variable) are covered by revenue and the business is making neither profits nor losses but is moving into a situation of profitability. The higher the fixed cost, the longer it takes to reach breakeven and profitability. A break-even analysis is not as complicated as it sounds. To carry out a break-even analysis, you need the following information:

• fixed costs per year
• variable costs per unit
• average price per unit.

Fixed costs are costs which do not change from month to month regardless of the units produced or sold. These may include equipment, administrative salaries, rent or mortgage payments, insurance etc. Variable costs are costs that change with the quantity of products manufactured or sold or services provided. Variable costs may include direct labour, raw materials, sales commissions, delivery expenses etc. Make sure you understand the difference between fixed and variable costs because in some businesses they are difficult to define.

The basic formula for break-even analysis is as follows:

$$BEQ = FC + NP/(P–VC)$$

BEQ = Break-even quantity
FC = Total fixed costs
NP = Net profit per annum
P = Average price per unit
VC = Variable costs per unit
P–VC = Contribution margin

Example

Sticking with our example above, your textile company (B. Smart Ltd) has fixed costs of £130,000 per annum. If your variable costs for each garment manufactured are £60 for materials and labour, you plan to sell each garment for £80, and the net profit is £28,000 for taking the risk of setting up the business, then how many units do you have to sell to break even?

Example 7.1: calculation of break-even point

$$\text{Break-even quantity} = \frac{\text{Fixed costs} + \text{Net profit}}{\text{Selling price} - \text{Variable costs}}$$

$$= \frac{130,000 + 28,000}{80 - 60} = 7,900 \text{ units}$$

Thus, in order to break even, you must sell 7,900 units of garments per annum at £80 each. If you decide to lower the selling price to £70 per garment, you will need to sell 15,800 units per annum in order to break even.

An alternative approach is to think in terms of the gross profit. Suppose you are aiming for 20% gross profit margin using the same equation:

$$\text{Breakeven} = \frac{130,000 + 28000}{0.2} = £790,000 \text{ turnover}$$

Ask yourself: can this be done? Estimate the effect of the following events on your break-even point each month:

10% rise or fall in sales volume
10% rise or fall in the unit selling price
10% rise or fall in variable costs
10% rise or fall in fixed costs.

Assume you have to achieve your profit objective by the end of year one. What volume of sales is required to break even? If necessary, try other percentages in order to obtain an understanding of how your business will behave under various conditions.

Ratio analysis

Ratio analysis is a form of financial statement which shows a quick indication of a firm's financial performance in key areas. Key financial ratios include the following:

(1)   Liquidity ratio

The liquidity ratio indicates the ability of a company to pay off both its current liabilities as they become due and its long-term liabilities as they become current. In other words, it shows the cash level of a company and its ability to turn current assets into cash to pay off current liabilities. The liquidity of a company measures how much cash a business has as well as how easy it is for the company to convert assets into cash. Current assets such as debtors or accounts receivable and stocks are relatively easy for many companies to convert into cash in the short term. Therefore, these assets are all included in the liquidity calculation. The most common forms of liquidity ratios are discussed below.

(a)   Current ratio (efficiency ratio)

The current ratio is a liquidity ratio or efficiency ratio that measures a company's ability to pay off its short-term liabilities with its current assets. It is an important measure of liquidity because short-term liabilities are due within the next year. This means that a company has a very short period of time in order to raise the funds to pay for these liabilities. Current assets include cash at bank and in hand, debtors, and stock. Companies with larger amounts of current assets can quite easily pay off current liabilities when they become due without having to sell off long-term, revenue-generating assets.

The current ratio shows how easily the company will be able to pay off its current liabilities. This ratio expresses a company's current debt in terms of current assets. Therefore, a current ratio of 2:1 means that the company has twice more current assets than current liabilities. A higher current ratio is better for a company than a lower current ratio because it shows it can more easily make current debt payments without having to sell off fixed assets, which often means that the company is not making enough money to meet its debts as they fall due.

Formula

Current ratio = Current assets/Current liabilities

(usually expressed as 1:1 or 2:1; 2:1 is ideal)

Example

From our example above, the balance sheet shows £45,000 of current liabilities and £45,000 of current assets, what will be your current ratio?

Current Ratio: 45,000/45,000

Current Ratio = 1

Your current ratio is 1, which means that you have just enough current assets to pay off your current liabilities. Bank managers usually prefer a current ratio of at least 1:1 or 2:1, where all the current liabilities would be covered by the current assets.

(b)   Quick ratio (or acid test ratio)

The quick ratio is a liquidity ratio that measures the ability of a company to pay its current liabilities when they become due with only quick assets. Quick assets are current assets that can be converted to cash within 90 days or less. They include cash in hand and cash at bank, cash equivalents, debtors, or current accounts receivable.

If a company has enough quick assets to cover its total liabilities, the company is in a position to pay off its obligations without having to sell off its long-term assets. Selling off long-term assets in order to meet its debts will adversely affect the company's ability to generate revenues. It will also indicate to potential investors that the company cannot meet its current obligations or liabilities.

The higher the quick ratios, the more favourable it is for the company since it indicates that the company has more quick assets than current liabilities. A quick ratio of 1:1 shows that the company's quick assets are equal to its current assets, which means that the company can pay off its currents liabilities without having to sell any long-term assets. An acid test ratio of 2:1 indicates that the company's quick assets are twice as many as its current liabilities. Therefore, as the quick ratio increases, so does the liquidity of the company, which is a good sign not only to potential investors but also to your creditors who are interested in knowing whether they will be paid back on time.

Formula

Quick ratio = Current assets – (Stock + Work in progress)/Current liabilities

   (1:1 is the ideal)

Example

Using your balance sheet above, which includes the following current assets and current liabilities, what is your company's quick ratio?

- Stock: £12,000
- Debtors: £25,000
- Cash at bank: £8,000
- Total current assets: £45,000
- Current liabilities: £45,000

$$\text{Quick ratio} = \frac{£25,000 + £8,000}{£45,000}$$

Quick ratio = 0.73

Alternatively, it can be calculated as follows:

$$\text{Quick ratio} = \frac{£45,000 - £12,000}{£45,000}$$

Quick ratio = 0.73

You can see that in both calculations, your quick ratio is 0.73, which means that you can pay off only 73% of your current liabilities with your quick assets.

(2)   *Profitability ratio*

Profitability ratios show a company's ability to generate profits from its operations. They can be used by investors and creditors to judge whether a company is making enough operational profit from its assets. In a way, profitability ratios relate to efficiency ratios because they show how well a company is using its assets to generate profits. Key profitable ratios include the following:

(a)   *Gross profit margin*

Gross profit margin is a profitability ratio that compares the gross profit of a business to the sales. This ratio measures the profitability of a company. In other words, the gross profit margin is essentially the percentage mark-up on the cost of a commodity to cover expenses and profit in fixing the selling price.

Gross profit margin should not be confused with the net profit margin. Gross profit margin only considers the cost of goods sold in its calculation because it measures the profitability of selling stock, whilst net profit margin on the other hand takes other expenses into consideration.

Obviously, the higher the gross profit margin, the more profitable is the company. A high margin can be achieved either by buying the materials or stock very cheap or by marking up the goods higher. Marking up the good higher must be done carefully to ensure that it is competitive with what competitors are charging; otherwise, customers may be lost. A high gross profit margin means that a company will have more money to pay operating expenses such as salaries, lighting and heating, rents, telephone etc.

Formula

Gross profit margin = Gross profit/Sales (%)

(usually expressed as a percentage)

Example

Your profit and loss statement above contains the following information:

Sales: £120,000
Gross profit: £55,000
Calculate your gross profit margin.

$$\text{Gross profit margin} = \frac{£55,000 \times 100\%}{£120,000}$$

Gross profit margin = 46%

This is obviously a good gross profit margin, which means that after you pay for your stock, you will still have 46% of your sales revenue to cover your operating costs.

(b)   Return on capital employed

Return on capital employed, or ROCE, is a profitability ratio that measures how efficiently a company can generate profits from its capital employed by comparing profit before tax to capital employed. In other words, it shows investors how much in profits £1 of capital employed generates. ROCE is a long-term profitability ratio because it shows how effectively assets are performing while taking into consideration long-term financing. Capital employed refers to the total assets of a company less all current liabilities or stockholders' equity less long-term liabilities. Both equal the same figure.

Since the return on capital employed shows how much profit £1 of capital employed generates, therefore a higher percentage would be more favourable because it means that more profits are generated by £1 of capital employed. Investors are interested in the ratio to see how efficiently a company uses its capital employed as well as its long-term financing strategies.

Formula

Return on capital employed = Profit before tax/Capital employed (%)

Example

The profit and loss statement and the balance sheet above contain the following figures:

Profit before tax = £40,000
Capital employed = £130,000

Therefore:

$$\text{Return on capital employed} = \frac{£40,000 \times 100\%}{£130,000}$$

$$= 0.31 \text{ or } 31\%$$

This means that £1 of capital employed generates 31 pence of profits. Perhaps the company is not making good use of its assets. Obviously, a company that has a small amount of assets but a large amount of profits will have a higher return than a company with twice as many assets and the same profits.

(3) Gearing ratio

(a) Debt/equity ratio

This ratio compares a company's total debt to total equity. The debt to equity ratio shows the percentage of company financing that comes from debt providers (e.g. bank loans) and equity providers (e.g. shareholders). A higher debt to equity ratio indicates that more debt financing is used than equity financing.

A debt to equity ratio of 1:1 means that investors or shareholders and loan providers have an equal stake in the business. A lower debt to equity ratio is usually preferable as it implies a more financially stable business. A higher debt to equity ratio is often considered to be highly geared and therefore more risky to creditors and investors than a lower ratio as debt must be repaid to the lender with interest.

Formula

The debt to equity ratio is calculated by dividing total debts by total equity. It is considered a balance sheet ratio because all of the elements (debt and equity) are reported on the balance sheet.

Debt/equity ratio = Debt/Equity
(usually expressed as a ratio 1:1 or 2:1; the ideal is 1:1)

Example

Since B. Smart Ltd has equity of £100,000, but no long-term debt, the company has no gearing and therefore is not risky at all. However, suppose the company had a long-term debt of £200,000 from the bank; the debt to equity ratio would be as follows:

$$\text{Debt/equity ratio} = \frac{£200,000}{£100,000}$$
$$= 2$$

This means that the gearing position is 2:1, which is highly geared, and investors and creditors would certainly view this company as risky. It suggests that investors have not funded the business as much as creditors. It also suggests that investors are unwilling to fund the business because it is not performing well. However, in rare cases, bank managers and other funders may still provide funding to a company with a 2:1 gearing position, provided the company exhibits other favourable characteristics such as a strong management team, a good track record and experience.

(b)   Interest cover

This ratio measures a company's ability to make interest payments on its debt in time. In other words, it shows the number of times interest payments are covered by a company's profit before interests and tax. A creditor uses the interest cover ratio to decide whether a company is able to service additional debt. The higher this ratio, the better for the company!

Formula

Interest cover = Profit before tax and interests/Interest payments

(usually expressed in time)

Example

The profit before tax for B. Smart Ltd is £40,000, but it does not have any interest payments. Suppose the company made an interest payment of £10,000. B. Smart's interest cover ratio would be calculated as follows:

$$\text{Interest cover} = \frac{£40,000}{£10,000}$$
$$= 4 \text{ times}$$

This would mean that B. Smart has four times more earnings than its current interest payments. It would mean that the company can well afford to pay the interest on its debt as well as its principal payments. It also shows that the company's risk is low and the business is making enough money to meet its obligations.

Summary

- Start-up costs – details of what you are going to spend your money on in order to set up the business. These consist of capital expenditures as well as variable costs and other regular outgoings.
- Financial statements – consisting of cash flow forecasts, profit and loss accounts, and balance sheets (for at least three years).
- Break-even analysis – which shows when the business is likely to cover its costs by the available revenue: when will you pay off the loan and reach your target profit?
- Ratio analysis – to show a quick indication of the firm's financial performance in key areas (e.g. liquidity ratios, profitability ratios, return on capital employed, gearing ratio, interest cover etc.).

References

Burns, P. (2014) *New Venture Creation: A Framework for Entrepreneurial Start-Ups*, Palgrave Macmillan, London.
Deakins, D. and Freel, M. (2012) *Entrepreneurship and Small Firms*, sixth edition, McGraw-Hill, London.

8 Operations management

The operational plan does not only apply to manufacturing business, as many people think. You should understand that every business needs to plan for its operations. It assesses the business locations, the layouts, and their adequacy in relation to the facilities, equipment, machinery, fixtures and fittings you need to run the business.

Therefore, operations management or service operations simply refer to the control of the day-to-day running of the business. It concerns the activities and decisions which are needed for the efficient delivery of products and services. This is conceptualized by thinking of the business as a *system of activities* involving inputs, throughput, output and customer feedback. Particularly relevant for service sector businesses are the nature of 'back-office' and 'frontoffice' activities, planning and control systems, support systems (telephones, computers), layout of office/premises, job design, and customer service/quality control.

The main functions controlled by the service/operations manager are:

(1) *Inputs* – these will vary from business to business. If you are making something, you will need to buy raw materials. If you are providing a service, you still need to identify your main inputs; information, for example, is necessary to decide what events a tour operator will choose to promote. If you are hiring out dresses for parties, do you make them or buy them? What labour is needed? Usually, it is necessary for the operations manager to create an *inventory* of the inputs.

(2) *Throughput* – this is the heart of the system and is the process of turning the basic inputs into services/products to be sold to the customer. The operations manager will need to provide a *schedule of activities* to indicate what is to be done when, and who is to do it, usually on a daily basis, especially if shift work is involved. The *layout* of your office/business unit/manufactory will need to be planned and a diagram produced, showing where machines, computers, storerooms/shop layout

etc. will be located. A *critical path analysis* or *project management* techniques could be useful here.

(3) ***Output*** – this concerns getting the finished product or service to the customer via delivery, packaging, over-the-counter service, or whatever is necessary. Again, a *schedule of activities, delivery system, and invoicing system* is something the operations manager would be required to produce.

There is also a:

(4) ***Feedback loop*** – where the attitude of the customer to the service or product is measured to provide information that will affect the system and lead to changes if necessary. This is often thought of as part of the system of ***quality control.*** The operations manager will need to liaise with the marketing manager on this.

Quality control procedures, inventory and production methods, as well as materials and finished-goods purchasing methods are also included in the operations plan. It is difficult to generalize on this, and you will need to think carefully and decide how much of the above is required to make your business operate smoothly. Key elements to include are:

(a) an office/workshop diagram, showing the layout of the workplace and key elements (e.g. equipment, computers etc.)
(b) a schedule of activities/flow diagram showing what work gets done when (you may wish to apply critical path analysis here).
(c) Other pointers include:

Materials, services and sources of supply

What do you require?

- How much – quantities and costs?
- Who can supply these?
- What are their terms and conditions of sale?
- Why did you choose them?
- How are you going to control your stock controls?

Production

- Will you make or buy? Why?
- Describe your production process?

- What plant and equipment is required?
- What are their output limits?
- Provide a plan of your facilities, and show the flow of goods, materials etc. Are there any constrictions or bottlenecks?
- What support will you require?
- In what ways can you control quality and service?
- What is your maximum production?
- What is your minimum production for survival?
- What is your optimum production?

Legal and insurance issues

- Terms and conditions of sale
- Insurance for premises, stock and equipment, public liability
- Systems/procedures necessary for compliance with legal requirements (e.g. risk assessment for health and safety and food hygiene, if relevant)
- Licenses

Selling and sales management

- Who will sell your products?
- In what ways will you sell them?
- Who will make decision and monitor and control your sales effort?
- What sales activity targets have you set?
- What selling aids will you need and/or provide?
- What objections do you expect from customers?
- How long is the process from the customer becoming aware of the product or service to making the decision to buy, receiving the product or service, and finally paying for it?
- In what ways will you motivate your sales team?
- In what ways will you handle complaints?

Services and collection

- What services will you provide?
- In what ways can you monitor them?
- What arrangements have you made for collecting your money and controlling your cash flow?

Capacity planning

This is the process of determining the people, machines, and major physical resources (such as buildings) necessary to meet the production objectives of the organization. Your productivity should be calculated as follows:

Productivity = Outputs/Inputs

= Goods and services produced/Labour + Capital + Energy + Technology

Summary

Have you remembered to show how the business works on a day-to-day basis, including the following elements?

- Systems approach to the business process and critical points
- Locations
- Scheduling of activities for product/service delivery
- Technology/equipment, other facilities
- Quality control/communications
- Make use of diagrams and schedules

9 HR-related tasks and legal compliance

You need to consider the extent to which it is appropriate to incorporate a developed human resource management (HRM) function as part of your start-up strategy and business plan, particularly if you are starting as a sole trader and not expecting to employ other people immediately. However, you must remember that a business plan is not only for the present; it is for the future as well. HRM responsibilities include recruitment, overseeing training and development, motivation, evaluation and compensation. Although the 'people' aspects of any small business are crucial to success, many small businesses operate without a separate HRM function and associated formal processes. Unlike firms which have grown in size over time, the small business has few staff members and limited time for formal staff development, especially in its first few years. However, there are a number of HR-related tasks that will need attention as discussed below.

Job specifications

A job specification is a statement of the essential components of a job class, including a summary of the work to be performed, primary duties and responsibilities, and the minimum qualifications and requirements necessary to perform the essential functions of the job. A job specification describes the knowledge, skills, education, experience and abilities you believe are essential to performing a particular job. These are briefly explained below.

- **Knowledge and skills** – state the skills, knowledge and personal characteristics of individuals required for the job.
- **Education** – state what degrees, training or certifications are required for the position.
- **Experience** – the number of years of work experience required for the job.

Therefore, a job specification will include a description of owner-manager, each manager's/partner's role (if any), plus those of any additional staff employed, full or part time.

The preparation of curriculum vitae (CV)

A **curriculum vitae** is a Latin word for 'course of life'. It is a summary of your experience, skills and education. It is also known as a résumé, which is the French word for 'summary'.

You may need to update your existing CV if you had one already; otherwise, you need to prepare one. Your CV and those of the management team can go into the appendices.

Organizational functioning and management structure/culture

An organizational function and structure is one in which the organization is divided into smaller groups based on specialized functional areas, such as IT, finance or marketing. These specialized units report to a single authority, usually called top management or CEO. These specialized units contain personnel with various but related skills grouped by similarities. Top management is responsible for coordinating the efforts of each unit and meshing them together into a cohesive whole.

It is common for small businesses not to have a solid organizational structure. All employees in start-up companies can perform a range of tasks outside of their official job descriptions, and a good number of them have generous leeway in making decisions. Aside from that, all employees in a start-up generally know to whom they report, since it is usually a single person or group – the owner or partners. However, it is very important to have a formal organizational structure in place before your company grows so large that your workforce becomes unwieldy.

Most small businesses operate what is known as a flat organizational structure in which there are relatively few layers of management. In a flat structure, front-line employees are empowered to make a range of decisions on their own. Information flows from the top down and from the bottom up in a flat structure, meaning communication flows from top-level management to front-line employees and from front-line employees back to top-level management.

Although it is rare for most small firms to have a well-developed management structure, organizational structure is important for any growing company in order to provide guidance and clarity on specific human resources

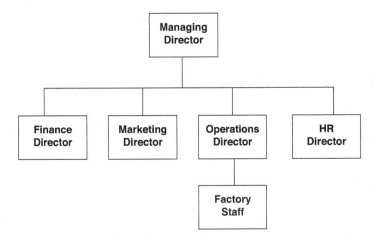

Figure 9.1 Example of a Simple Structure

issues, such as managerial authority. Small-business owners should therefore be encouraged to begin to think about a formal structure early in the growth stage of their business.

Organizational culture is also an important part of your organizational plan. It is a system of shared assumptions, values and beliefs which govern how people behave in organizations. These shared values have a strong influence on the people in the organization and dictate how they dress, act and perform their jobs.

Therefore, in preparing your business plan, you might need to answer the following questions: what are the different roles in your organization, and how do they interrelate? What is the management style/culture, i.e. emphasizing delegation and democratic decision-making or more hierarchical/autocratic? How are managers/staff to be motivated and rewarded for their efforts? What are the values that will underpin working relationships? If your start-up is a large one, an organization chart can go into this chapter.

Competencies and development

These involve the competency, knowledge, skills and attributes needed for people within an organization. Each individual role has its own set of competencies needed to perform the job effectively. To develop competencies in your business, you need to have an in-depth understanding of the roles within your business. To do this, you can take any of the following approaches:

- a pre-set list of common, standard competencies, and then customize it to the specific needs of your organization
- outside consultants to develop the framework for you
- create a general organizational framework, and use it as the basis for other frameworks as needed.

These approaches will result in the identification of existing competencies and any gaps and sourcing of learning opportunities, e.g. do you need 'informal' learning from other members of the business or through links to external sources of expertise? Do you need to send staff on any training courses, such as IT or other skills needed for the business? If so, remember to cost these out and include them in the start-up costs.

Recruitment and selection

Recruitment is the process of identifying that the organization needs to employ someone up to the point at which application forms for the post have been successfully designed. Selection then consists of the processes involved in choosing, from a pool of applicants, a suitable candidate to fill a post.

If you need to recruit a staff or additional staff, you will be responsible for the preparation of advertisements (be aware of the equal opportunities legislation). You will need to ascertain the cost of such adverts if they need to be included as start-up costs. You need also to ascertain the recruitment criteria.

In order to ensure efficiency in the recruitment and selection process, the following steps can be suggested:

- identify vacancy and evaluate need
- develop position description
- develop recruitment plan
- select search committee (if appropriate)
- advertise position and implement recruitment plan
- review applicants and develop a short list
- conduct interviews
- select hire
- finalize recruitment.

Reward system

Another aspect of the HR-related task is the reward system. How do you intend to motivate and reward your staff? Employee reward systems refer to programs set up by a company to reward performance and motivate employees on individual and/or group levels. They are normally considered separate from salary but may be monetary in nature or otherwise have a cost to the company. This includes bonuses, profit sharing etc. and emphasizes excellence or achievement rather than basic competency. While previously considered the domain of large companies, small businesses have also begun employing them as a tool to lure top employees in a competitive job market as well as to increase employee performance.

Legislation

Start-up owners/managers are responsible for knowing which aspects of the law impinge on their business, including employment and health and safety law (often the responsibility of the HRM function in larger businesses). You will need to identify which laws apply to your business and what measures, policies and actions you need to take in order to be compliant. The usual legislations which are applicable to most small businesses are:

- **Employment law** – employment law and employee legislation in Britain are to protect the work force against discrimination from co-workers and employers. Employment protection refers to regulations concerning both hiring (e.g. rules favouring disadvantaged groups, conditions for using temporary or fixed-term contracts, training requirements) and firing (including redundancy procedures, mandated pre-notification periods and severance payments, special requirements for collective dismissals and short-time work schemes).
- **Health and safety legislation** – this is a piece of legislation covering the workplace (e.g. Health and Safety at Work Act 1974). The Health and Safety at Work Act 1974 is the primary piece of legislation covering occupational health and safety in Great Britain. The health and safety executive, with local authorities (and other enforcing authorities), is responsible for enforcing the act and a number of other acts and statutory instruments relevant to the working environment.
- **Hygiene law (food and safety)** – food hygiene legislation affects all food businesses that regularly produce, handle, transport, process or supply food. This includes caterers, primary producers (such as farmers), manufacturers and retailers. How it affects you will depend on the nature of your business.

Some of these considerations may also need to be integrated with the day-to-day operational aspects of the business, for instance with respect to health and safety procedures. Again, it is difficult to generalize, so make sure you only create tasks related to HR which are necessary to the business start-up. Please do not include large sections derived from HRM textbooks which are more relevant to the HRM function in large firms. You do not need to quote vast chunks of law – the key point is to demonstrate that you are aware of the requirements and to show how you will comply.

If you have a management team, you should be looking at the intra- and interpersonal qualities of the management team. A management team with an established track record in the industry and relevant experience will certainly add credibility to your business. Remember that investors ultimately invest in people and not products.

Summary

- Describe management personnel and their positions, expertise and roles.
- Management structure/organizational culture – name your management team (if any) and organizational chart if the structure of the business is too complex.
- Discuss any development/training needs, supervisory procedures and costs.
- Reward systems – explain the compensation methods and levels as well as employment contracts and partnership agreements.
- Recruitment – show the number of employees you will need as well as their tasks and methods of employment and pay.
- Discuss relevant legislations, how they affect your business and how you will comply with this. Discuss also patents, trade secrets and any other legal contracts that apply to your business, including licenses and permits.

10 Risk analysis, growth and exit planning

Business risk analysis is part of the planning process. It reveals all the hidden hazards which occupy the business owner's mind on a subconscious level but which have not been carefully considered and documented on a conscious level.

Risk and 'worry' are intrinsically linked. By identifying the risks which lie ahead, we reduce the worry and help bring about a more balanced working environment. Knowing what is coming up around the corner is very important in promoting a more stable and confident working environment. This includes:

- high level of competition
- political deadlock
- tax policies
- interest rates
- inflation
- consumer sentiment
- economic uncertainty
- geopolitical issues that were never even discussed before
- unemployment
- rising healthcare costs
- technological advancement.

For this reason, exit planning should always be an integral part of your big plan, and it will pay huge dividends if you begin your preparations early. An exit strategy is a planned approach to terminating your business in a way that will maximize benefit and/or minimize damage. You need to ask yourself the following questions when considering exit planning:

- How much money do you need to enjoy the lifestyle you expect when you retire?

- What kind of company will be interested in acquiring your business (is it just a hunch you have, or have you examined the possibilities scientifically)?
- Are you clear about what potential buyers will be looking for when you come to market your business?
- Have you created a strategy to maximize your company's equity value to ensure that you achieve the highest possible sale price?
- Do you know the different options open to you when you come to sell your business?
- Are you aware of how to market your business so that you maximize your exposure to potential buyers?

Exit planning is about controlling how and when you exit your business, while maximizing value, reducing risk, and preserving wealth. Whether you intend to transfer the business to family, management or a third party, an exit plan produces a more successful exit. Getting your head around your proposed exit route has significant practical benefits too. It is far more enjoyable (and less stressful) to run a business which has a clear sense of direction and common purpose.

The benefits of an exit plan include more and better buyers, a higher price, less in taxes, and a trouble-free leadership transfer. An exit plan also clears and settles your mind, re-energizes you and gives your work greater purpose. It focuses your attention and reduces your stress and anxiety. The benefits of exit planning can be summarized as follows:

- clarifies your best transfer option and timing
- identifies value and marketability gaps
- increases shareholder value
- positions the company to attract more and better buyers
- ensures business continuity
- makes ownership transfer more seamless
- increases cash proceeds
- minimizes taxes
- minimizes financial risk
- prevents costly mistakes.

There are some steps you must follow in exit planning. The first step in the exit planning process is an objective analysis of business value, transferability and marketability. This involves:

- reviewing company operations, history, markets, customers, suppliers, competition, management, systems, documentation, tangible and intangible assets etc.

- financial performance analysis
- financial statement quality
- comparison to the industry
- SWOT analysis
- properly applying accepted business valuation methods
- considering appropriate premiums and discounts
- value (a number or range)
- tests for reasonableness
- likely buyers, deal structures, financing
- marketability factor analysis, and obstacle identification
- insight into enhancement opportunities.

The second step is the planning phase. The planning phase starts with selecting your best exit option(s) and timeframe. When a third-party sale is your preferred option, the plan prepares you and the business for the selling process. In a nutshell you have four principle options when you eventually come to transfer your business interests. You may:

- transfer ownership to your children
- sell the business to other owners or employees
- sell to a third party
- liquidate.

Summary

- Identify the risks associated with your business.
- Point out your exit strategies.

11 Conclusion

In this chapter, you need to state clearly the purpose of the business plan. If it is for the purposes of raising a loan or other forms of funding, you have to say so and state the amount needed and how it will be repaid (interest and principal) monthly. You also have to state on what the loan will be secured and the value of the collateral.

You need to summarize the case for the business: why do you think it will be successful, and how has this been demonstrated in the business plan? As the chief executive of the business, you need to emphasize your strong profile and commitment to the success of the business – planning and supervising the entire operation, selecting and training all employees to perform the necessary sales and creative production functions, scheduling all daily work assignments, and developing cost estimates and a cost-effective promotional advertising plan.

Your conclusion should tell your readers why your business plan should matter to them after they finish reading it. The conclusion gives you the opportunity to have the last word or the final say on your business plan – on the important issues you have raised in the plan. It allows you to synthesize your business ideas and to demonstrate the importance of your ideas. Your conclusion should give your readers something to take away that will help them to form a good impression of your business. It is therefore an opportunity for you to make a good final impression and to end your business plan on a positive note.

In writing your conclusion, it is important to keep asking yourself the 'so what' question: why should anyone care about your business idea? Why should they be interested in investing in your business? In writing the conclusion, it can be helpful to return to your introductory paragraph and to read through the body of your business plan one more time to be acquainted with the key words and concepts which you used earlier in the business plan.

It is worth bearing in mind that the conclusion is not a repetition of the executive summary or any part of the business plan. Your conclusion should be interesting and make your readers happy that they read your plan. Therefore, the conclusion of your plan should have a significant influence on your readers.

Avoid beginning your conclusion with phrases such as 'in conclusion', 'in summary' or 'in closing'. Although there is nothing terribly wrong with those phrases, they are unnecessary and have been overused. It is also necessary to avoid concluding your business plan with a sentimental or emotional appeal which has little or no bearing with the content of your plan.

Appendices

Appendix 1

Example of finding a gap in the market: Tony Stone and Stoats Porridge Bars

Tony Stone is a young entrepreneur who graduated from university with a marketing degree. However, after working in the tourism industry for a short time at a small hotel, he returned to his home in Edinburgh, determined to find a means of independent employment, working for himself – the enterprise.

While at home looking for alternative employment, Tony found a lot of attention on the health advantages of one of his native country's former national dishes: porridge. Newspapers featured articles from health experts on the nutritional benefits of porridge, including lowering cholesterol. Articles commented that porridge, after years in the doldrums, had seen a recent reversal with sales increasing by 24% in the previous year. This gave an informational cue to Tony which started him thinking about the ways that porridge could be made attractive. He decided to experiment with making porridge oat bars, but with modern flavours such as cranberry and macadamia nuts. In 2005, Tony and his business partner, Bob Arnott, were successful in getting a small start-up loan from the Prince's Scottish Youth Business Trust and a small start-up grant. However, these combined were insufficient to launch the business on any scale, and his first sales were generated from taking a selection of porridge oat bars in a second-hand trailer (bought with his initial start-up finance) to a series of festivals around the UK, including events such as Glastonbury and 'T in the Park'. In addition he was able to target smaller events such as farmers' markets at different locations throughout the UK. By 2007, the initial success at different events had provided the means for Tony to acquire sufficient resources to move into larger-scale production and to diversify by opening his first Stoats Porridge Bar in Edinburg, selling flavoured porridge, including apple, chocolate and roasted hazelnuts – a healthy alternative to other forms of fast food.

Source: Deakins and Freel (2012)

Appendix 2

Example of turning a hobby into a business: Lawton Dancewear

Lesley Holland's daughter decided she wanted to be a dancer about six years ago – not an uncommon ambition for a 9-year-old girl! Her career started with ballet and tap classes and included, eventually, Irish dancing. At this point, Lesley, who had a family to support, noticed that her daughter's current passion was beginning to impact on her purse strings.

Irish dancing costumes are expensive and (as Lesley's family was based in the rural Borders region between England and Scotland) had to be bought either by mail order from Ireland or via a visit to Coatbridge, near Glasgow – Scotland's only Irish dance dressmaker at that time. A keen hobby seamstress, Lesley decided it would be easier and less expensive if she were to make her daughter's costumes herself.

The first Irish dance dress Lesley made for her daughter was a huge success. Not only was her daughter delighted with it, but her friends and, more importantly, her friends' parents were also impressed. Increasingly, friends and neighbours in the Borders town of Galashiels who had children in Irish dancing classes asked Lesley if she could make their dresses too. Working from home, and with no industrial machinery, Lesley supplied local people with dresses for the cost of materials and pin money. When the volume of work increased, Lesley was only too glad to be able to take some help in the form of Lynn, a student of textile at a local university, doing part-time experience placement. Lesley was in business!

Source: Deakins and Freel (2012)

Appendix 3
Business plan template

Cover sheet

Table of contents

1. Executive summary

1.1 Business profile

Summarize briefly the contents of the business profile section.

1.2 Marketing plan

Summarize briefly the contents of the marketing plan section.

1.3 Operations plan

Summarize briefly the contents of the operations plan section

1.4 Risk assessment

Summarize briefly the contents of the risk assessment section

1.5 Financial plan

Summarize briefly the contents of the financial plan section

2. Business profile

Include a brief introduction to this section; tell the readers what they may expect from this section.

2.1 A description of the industry

Briefly describe the industry sector of your business. What business are you in? What are the related industries? What are the trends for your industry? Is it growing, mature or declining? Are there any technological, economic or social factors that will affect your business in the near future?

2.2 A description of the business products or services

Briefly describe the products or services your business provides. Include a mission statement here.

2.3 A description of the location

Briefly describe the location, and explain the advantages of this location. State why you have chosen this location. Describe the layout of the premises, and include in an appendix a floor plan of your business.

2.4 The legal structure

Describe the legal structure for the business, and explain why you have chosen this structure. If it is a partnership or a company, provide details of the agreements or articles. Detail any statutory and regulatory requirements for your business.

2.5 Issues analysis of the business

Detail the various factors both negative and positive that will influence and impact on your business. You need to think about your own abilities and skills that you either have or do not have. Explain what each of these means for your business.

2.6 A description of the business objectives

Detail the business objectives, including personal, financial, marketing and operational objectives. Briefly describe the future direction you envisage for your business. Include a brief vision statement here.

3. Marketing plan

Include a brief introduction to this section; tell the readers what they may expect from this section.

3.1 Features and benefits of the products and services

Describe the features and benefits of each product or service. Explain what the customer is buying.

3.2 Customer profile

Describe your customers. Include demographic, social, behavioural and any other information about your customers. Link this profile to the features and benefits of your products or services.

3.3 Competitor analysis

Describe your competitors. What are their strengths and weaknesses? Where are they located? What do they sell?

3.4 Competitive advantage

Describe how you will be different from your competitors. Link this to your competitor analysis and customer profile.

3.5 Advertising and promotional activities

Explain how you will tell your customers about your business. What activities will you undertake to entice customers to buy your products or services? Explain how you will monitor your response rate. Include a schedule for your advertising and promotional activities. Explain how your advertising and promotional activities fit your customer profile and features and benefits

3.6 Pricing method

How will you price your products or services? Explain why you have chosen that method.

3.7 Selling and distribution method

What method of selling or distribution will you use? Explain why you have chosen that method.

4. Operations plan

Include a brief introduction to this section; tell the readers what they may expect from this section.

4.1 Operating processes

What equipment do you need? What equipment do you have already? Explain how you can use this equipment to provide the products or services you will sell. What operating processes will you use? How will you monitor output? Include a brief flow chart to demonstrate the processes. How will you store stock? What levels of inventory will you keep? How will you keep track of your inventory?

4.2 Suppliers

Who are your suppliers? Why have you chosen them? How will you pay them?

4.3 Management team

Describe the management team. Use job descriptions and selection criteria for each member of the management team. Describe how you will measure their performance.

4.4 Staff

Provide job descriptions and selection criteria for each staff member. Describe how you will recruit staff. Provide a simple application form for staff. Describe how you will measure their performance.

4.5 Key personnel

List key personnel you may call on for business advice. Explain why you have chosen them and how you will pay them.

4.6 Record keeping

Describe records you will keep for your business.

5. Risk assessment

Include a brief introduction to this section; tell the readers what they may expect from this section.

5.1 Industry risk assessment

Describe the risks of entering this industry and business sector. What factors can affect your business? Detail initial start-up costs and where you will get this money.

5.2 Existing skills assessment

Explain the missing skills you may have in terms of both industry experience and business management skills.

5.3 Business structure assessment

Identify the weaknesses and threats in your business processes, including your marketing plan. Detail the demographics. Detail the technological requirements. Detail uncontrollable factors.

5.4 Risk mitigation

Detail the risk mitigation in terms of the above factors. Explain how you intend to reduce the risks you face.

6. Financial plan

Include a brief introduction to this section; tell the readers what they may expect from this section

6.1 Projected ratios

Describe the various ratios you have used to assess the profitability and return on investment for business.

6.2 Projected cash flow

Describe the projected cash flow for this business. Explain why you have made the assumptions that you have. If you have an operating loss, explain how you will fund this.

6.3 Projected profit and loss

Describe the projected profit and loss for this business. Explain why you have made the assumptions that you have. If you have an operating loss, explain how you will fund this.

6.4 Projected balance sheet

Describe the projected balance sheet for this business. Explain why you have made the assumptions that you have.

6.5 Spreadsheets

Provide projected cash flow, profit and loss, and balance sheet spreadsheets for three years

Appendix 4

Sample business plan (1) – WorldFood Enterprises

Director
Mr Joe Paris

REGISTERED ADDRESS
2017 RUE DE L'EXPOSITION, PARIS

Executive summary

WorldFood Enterprises (WorldFood) is a food company based in Paris that distributes basic food directly to the end user. We sell rice, pasta, semolina, farina, beans, cooking oil and other essential commodities.

Although these items are already found in many shops, our unique selling point is that we target large households: we sell in bulk, and we deliver to the doorstep. By doing so, we develop in our customers a sense of belonging which brings about loyalty.

The food industry is a huge market, everybody buys our products, the gross margin is around 40%, and we expect to break even before the end of the first year of business.

WorldFood will develop a marketing tool which is new and unique to the business: the 'Active Word of Mouth', which consists of getting our customers to advertise out products. By doing so, they attract a good discount on their own purchases.

The business is operating from its registered address at 2017 Rue de l'Exposition, Paris.

The legal status of the company is 'Societe A Responsabilite Limitee' (which is equivalent to the UK 'Private Limited Company') and is owned by one director – namely Mr Joe Paris, who is the Managing Director.

Contents

- Business name
- Legal form

2. Business strategy

- Vision
- Mission statement
- Aims and objectives
- SWOT analysis
- Location
- Directors names and addresses

3. Marketing/market research

- Market size
- Target market
- Competitors
- Primary research analysis
- Advertising and promotion strategies
- Selling strategies

4. Finance

- Start-up costs
- Pricing strategy
- Payments by clients
- Projected cash flow
- Projected profit and loss account and balance sheet
- Break-even analysis
- Other finance ratios

5. Operations management

- Premises and layout
- Equipment
- Sources of supply
- Customer service
- Production process

6. Human resources management

- Organizational chart/management style
- Key people and their functions
- Background details of directors
- Recruitment procedure
- Training

7.   Risk assessment

- Risk management
- Exit strategy

8.   Conclusion

1.   Introduction

1.1   Business history

The purpose of this business plan is to illustrate our business idea and to prove to potential investors that we have a solid business plan in place with potential for high returns on capital. The plan can also be used by World-Food to secure some funding when needed.

WorldFood is a food company based in Paris. We distribute basic food directly to the end user. We sell rice, pasta, semolina, farina, beans, cooking oil and other essential commodities.

We chose to go into the food business in order to turn our experience into a business and to be in a position to make good money. The industry is relatively stable in the sense that there will always be demand for food; therefore, we believe that we will flourish in this industry.

We have explored and identified potential customers through market research. Our market research shows that Paris contains a large population of people, such as professionals and working-class citizens. We feel that all sections of the population will benefit from our business as our food items are sold at reasonable and affordable prices.

1.2   Business name

The name of the business is WorldFood Enterprises.

1.3   Legal form

The business is incorporated as 'Societe A Responsabilite Limitee', the equivalent of a limited liability company in the UK. As a limited liability company, the liability of the directors and potential shareholders is limited to the amount of capital that each of them has invested in the company. This form of incorporation will make the company more attractive to investors, customers and suppliers. The downside to this is the need to comply with more regulations, tax, and greater disclosure of information.

2.   Business strategy

2.1   Vision

The vision of the company is to improve the quality of life of the people by providing them with high-quality food and by making our impact felt in the local community and throughout the nation.

2.2   Mission statement

Our aim is to provide very high-quality food to the nation. We aim to be the best by providing a flourishing working environment for our employees. We also aim at putting something back into our local community and providing high-quality food for less.

2.3   Aims and objectives

Short-term objectives

- To gain a foothold in the food market by selling our products to at least 10% of families of African origin, which is our niche market.
- To establish a good reputation among customers and to excel in customer satisfaction.
- To gain a competitive edge over rival food sellers.

Long-term objectives

- To expand within France and become an established and well-known food company in the next ten years.
- To expand into other European markets (such as the UK and Germany) and the USA.
- To diversify our products into all varieties of foods.
- To increase our customer base by at least 20% each year.
- To develop a sustainable and profitable business.

2.4   SWOT analysis

Table A4.2.1 SWOT Analysis

Strengths	Weaknesses
• Unique formula	• Lack of experience in the industry
• User-marketer policy	• Limited advertisement budget
• Conviviality	
• Organized customer loyalty	

(*Continued*)

Table A4.2.1 (Continued)

Opportunities	Threats
• Possibility to expand to other areas	• No barrier to potential entrants
• Possibility to develop staff skills and knowledge through training	• Competition may use their financial power to lower their prices in order to
• Opportunity to add new lines of products	suffocate us
• We may be able to turn our customers into small distributors, which should help expand the market and also strengthen loyalty	

Strengths

- We have a unique formula which consists of taking the business directly to the customer. We deliver the items, seeking to become their appointed supplier.
- We will also bring a user-marketer policy into this market. This is based on our customers telling others about our products, which earns them an incentive from every customer they recruit, down to the third generation.
- This policy will bring a high level of loyalty as it will cultivate a good sense of belonging.

Weaknesses

- This is a new business, and we are stepping into an unknown field. Therefore, the lack of experience is the challenge. But this is a new concept. It is our concept. So it is our duty to be at work and learn as quickly as possible. We will then become pace setters.

Opportunities

- We may be able to turn our customers into small distributors. Those who will have introduced a huge number of customers could graduate to working as partners, especially in some remote areas where the distribution costs could be too challenging.

Threats

- There are no barriers to potential entrants. Our concept can be easily copied, especially by people who have greater financial power than we do. We would then find it hard to compete. Therefore, we have to work hard on customer loyalty, through outstanding customer service.

2.5   Location

The business is located at 2017 Rue de l'Exposition, Paris.

2.6   Directors names and addresses

Mr Joe Paris – Managing Director: No. 123, Joe Paris Avenue, Paris.

3.   Marketing/market research

3.1   Market size

The basic food market in France is huge. In 2010, 240,000 tons of rice were consumed in France. In value, this amounts to 480 million euros. In addition, 505,000 tons of pasta were consumed, which is around 874 million euros. Almost everyone (90% of the population) consumes the food that we sell.

The average person consumed 8kg of pasta in 2010. This consumption is increasing by 4% a year, causing the prices to rise by 10.8% between 2008 and 2009. In the same period, rice went up in price by 17%. The average person consumed 1.7kg in 1960 and 4.5kg in 2010. By 2014, this figure had risen to 7kg.

3.2   Target market

Our market is the whole of the French population, although our target market is the families of African descent. They make up around 220,000 households, and their consumption is 30% to 50% above the national average.

3.3   Competitors analysis

We have three levels of competition:

The first level of competition is the retail stores. All the big retail stores are partakers in this market. The big brands are Carrefour, Leclerc, Auchan, Franprix and Geant. Their trading area is national, and they represent 56% of the market. Our core products do not seem to attract competition between these stores.

They are mostly located in big shopping centres and ensure that they are distant to one another. With thousands of products on offer, it becomes hard to compare, and nobody buys their 1kg package of rice from one store and

Table A4.3.1 Competitors Analysis

General Description	Competition A	Competition B	Competition C	Worldfood
	Supermarkets	Local grocers	Open market	
Products				
Semolina	Yes	Yes	Yes	Yes
Farina	Yes	Yes	Yes	Yes
Rice	Yes	Yes	Yes	Yes
Attieke	No	No	Yes	Yes
Gary	No	No	Yes	Yes
Couscous	Yes	Yes	Yes	Yes
Pasta	Yes	Yes	Yes	Yes
Cooking Oil	Yes	Yes	Yes	Yes
Beans	Yes	Yes	Yes	Yes
Pricing strategy	According to internal competition	20–30% higher than A	Cheaper than the retail stores	Cheaper or as cheap as the cheapest
Promotional strategy	General advertisement	None	None	Active Word of Mouth, loyalty bonus scheme
Distribution	Local supermarket	Corner shops	Open market	Home delivery

then walks a mile to the next store to pick up their 1kg package of pasta. Basmati perfumed rice is sold at 2.93 euros at Carrefour and 3.33 euros at Geant. This is 13.65% more expensive than Carrefour.

5kg of couscous is sold at 8.52 euros at Carrefour and 7.73 euros at Geant. This is 9.6% cheaper than Carrefour.

A 5kg bag of semolina is sold at 6.30 euros at Carrefour and 5.94 euros at Geant. This is 6.34% cheaper.

This level of competition is found in some big retail stores which have huge marketing power. Their weakness is that our core business is only one of their thousands of products.

The second level of competition is the corner shops. They are known to be more expensive than the big retail stores. Nevertheless, their location is their unique selling point. They are not places one will visit with a long shopping list; their customers are people who are missing only one or two things and who are not going to walk a few more yards to save a few cents. Conviviality is also their strength. Oftentimes, the customers know the shopkeeper by name. The corner shop becomes a family shop.

The third level of competition is the ethnic products market. The main market of this kind in Paris is the Chateau Rouge market, where many Asian and African shops are concentrated. They are slightly cheaper than the big retail outlets. A 5 kg bag of semolina is 5 euros on average: 1 euro a kilo! This is 20% cheaper than Carrefour or 15.8% cheaper than Geant. Rice and couscous are sold almost at the same price as at Geant. Sunflower cooking oil is sold at 2.50 euros a litre, which is 16% cheaper than Geant and 7.4% cheaper than Carrefour.

3.4 Primary research analysis

We sell essential commodities which everybody consumes in almost every meal. So our focus is not about who will want our product but on who could buy from us the way we do things.

In our primary research, 1,000 people were questioned about their buying intentions. They were asked if they would buy from WorldFood: 80% of respondents who were members of large families said 'yes' they would certainly buy from us, while only 20% indicated that they had no such intention, but maybe. This shows a very high proportion of potential buyers.

Only 40% of respondents who were members of small-size families said they would certainly buy from us; 40% said they would not bother; while 20% said maybe.

The 40% who said they would not bother explained that they were not big eaters and could not see themselves buying a 10kg bag of semolina that would last them six to seven months. The interview also revealed a concern about not having available cash on the day of delivery. We have responded to this concern by setting up a Customer Credit Policy as detailed further below in the Customer Service section of chapter 5.

3.5 Advertising and promotion

We will make buyers aware of our products in various ways as discussed below:

Flyers – we will share flyers at selected locations such as churches, mosques, train stations, marketplaces, betting shops etc. These flyers will be handed to potential customers after qualifying them. We want to know the buying power of everyone to whom we hand flyers. So we talk to them, share flyers, take their details and follow up to close the deal.

Radio – we will participate in some radio programmes in order to promote WorldFood and its products.

Newspapers – we will advertise in some newspapers, especially those accepting free advertisements.

Website – we will have a website which will allow potential customers to get to know us and also place orders.

3.6   Selling strategies

- *Delivery*

We will put in place a delivery system which will lead us to cover one department after the other and one region after another. On every order, we will encourage the customers to fill up their 'basket' as much as possible. The basket is what makes up the order – i.e. 20kg of rice, 10 kg of semolina and 5kg of beans. We aim to have baskets of around 100 euros in order to minimize the delivery cost, which we estimate at 12 euros. This delivery is financed by our gross margin, which we estimate at 48%. The delivery cost enters in the calculation of cost of goods sold.

- *Warehouse pick up*

Although direct distribution is our policy, our customers will be able to get supply directly from the warehouse and earn themselves a discount for saved delivery costs. In the long run, we will multiply these distribution centres.

4.   Finance

4.1   Start-up costs

To start up, the company needs a minimum of 20,000 euros, which is to be used for the following items listed in the table below:

Table A4.4.1 Start-Up Costs and Expenditure

Start-up costs	Euros
Warehouse	1,200
Van	5,000
Furniture	300
IT equipment	1,000
Inventory	1,0000
Legal fees	2,000
Other expenses	500
Total	20,000

4.2   Pricing strategy

Customers are attracted to a particular business for a variety of reasons, and one of them is how much they will spend when they come to us. Pricing strategy refers to the method used by a company to set prices of their products or services. Almost all companies, large or small, base the price of their products or services on production (or acquisition), labour and advertising expenses and then add on a certain percentage so they can make a profit. There are several different pricing strategies such as penetration pricing, price skimming, discount pricing and competitive pricing, etc.

- *Penetration pricing*

A small company that uses penetration pricing typically sets a low price for its products or services in the hope of building market share, which is the percentage of sales a company has in the market versus total sales. The primary objective of penetration pricing is to garner lots of customers with low prices and then use various marketing strategies to retain them.

- *Price skimming*

Another type of pricing strategy is price skimming in which a company sets its prices high to quickly recover expenditures for product production (or acquisition) and advertising. The key objective of a price skimming strategy is to achieve a profit quickly. Companies often use price skimming when they lack financial resources to produce products in volumes.

- *Competitive-based pricing*

There are times when a small company may have a lower price to meet the prices of competitors. A competitive-based pricing strategy may be employed when there is little difference between products in an industry.

- *Temporary discount pricing*

Small companies also may use temporary discounts to increase sales. Temporary discount pricing strategies include coupons, cents-off sales, seasonal price reductions and even volume purchases.

- *WorldFood's pricing strategy*

Our pricing strategy is a mixture of the above strategies. There is little difference between products in our industry. They are not performance-based or design-based products. Therefore, we have to meet the prices of our competitors. We will use penetration pricing for items that offer customers a certain choice. These are items like rice, where we have Basmati, Thailand etc. We sell our products in 'baskets' which contain a variety of items; a penetration pricing on one item will bring attraction for the whole basket. We will set our prices high enough to quickly recover expenditures, and at the same time we will offer discounts in order to increase our volume. We do this by offering incentives, as explained further below in the Customer Service section of chapter 5.

4.3 Projected cash flow

The cash flow forecasts shown below are projected from estimated quarterly sales totalling 86,400 euros in the first year; 302,400 euros in the second year; and 648,000 euros in the third year. It is assumed that the figures in the cash flow (both receipts and payments) will be relatively stable for the three years. The sales figure is assumed to increase in the second quarter by 50% and 33% in the third quarter. In the second year, the assumption is that sales will increase by about 29% in the second quarter and 22% in the third. In the third year, it is assumed that sales will increase by 20% in the second quarter and by 17% in the third.

Figures used in the cash flow calculations

We get 40 new customers every month. All customers make three purchases in a year.

Unit selling price	90

We assume all of our customers pay in two instalments: half in current month and the other half in the following month.

Direct cost of unit sold	58
Purchases	46
Delivery	12

Table A4.4.2 WorldFood Enterprises Cash Flow Forecast for Year 1 (in Euros)

	Apr	May	Jun	Jul	Aug	Sept	Oct	Nov	Dec	Jan	Feb	Mar	Total
Receipts													
Bal b/f	0	8,655	7,310	5,965	4,620	4,555	4,490	4,425	4,360	5,575	6,790	8,005	
Starting cash	10,000	0	0	0	0	0	0	0	0	0	0	0	10,000
Sales	3,600	3,600	3,600	3,600	7,200	7,200	7,200	7,200	10,800	10,800	10,800	10,800	86,400
Total	13,600	12,255	10,910	9,565	11,820	11,755	11,690	11,625	15,160	16,375	17,590	18,805	96,400
Payments													
Cost of sales	2,320	2,320	2,320	2,320	4,640	4,640	4,640	4,640	6,060	6,960	6,960	6,960	55,680
Indirect costs	2,625	2,625	2,625	2,625	2,625	2,625	2,625	2,625	2,625	2,625	2,625	2,625	31,500
Total	4,945	4,945	4,945	4,945	7,265	7,265	7,265	7,265	9,585	9,585	9,585	9,585	87,180
Bal c/f	8,655	7,310	5,965	4,620	4,555	4,490	4,425	4,360	5,575	6,790	8,005	9,220	

Table A4.4.3 WorldFood Enterprises Cash Flow Forecast for Year 2 (in Euros)

	Apr	May	Jun	Jul	Aug	Sept	Oct	Nov	Dec	Jan	Feb	Mar	Total
Receipts													
Bal b/f	9,220	12,095	14,970	17,845	20,720	26,155	31,590	37,025	42,460	50,455	58,450	66,445	
Sales	18,000	18,000	18,000	18,000	25,200	25,200	25,200	25,200	32,400	32,400	32,400	32,400	302,400
Total	27,220	30,095	32,970	35,845	45,920	51,355	56,790	62,225	74,860	82,855	90,850	98,845	
Payments													
Cost of sales	11,600	11,600	11,600	11,600	16,240	16,240	16,240	16,240	20,880	20,880	20,880	20,880	194,880
Indirect costs	3,525	3,525	3,525	3,525	3,525	3,525	3,525	3,525	3,525	3,525	3,525	3,525	42,300
Total	15,125	15,125	15,125	15,125	19,765	19,765	19,765	19,765	24,405	24,405	24,405	24,405	237,180
Bal c/f	12,095	14,970	17,845	20,720	26,155	31,590	37,025	42,460	50,455	58,450	66,445	74,440	

Table A4.4.4 WorldFood Enterprises Cash Flow Forecast for Year 3 (in Euros)

	Apr	May	Jun	Jul	Aug	Sept	Oct	Nov	Dec	Jan	Feb	Mar	Total
Receipts													
Bal b/f	74,440	85,375	96,310	107,245	118,180	132,955	147,730	162,505	177,280	195,895	214,510	233,125	
Sales	43,200	43,200	43,200	43,200	54,000	54,000	54,000	54,000	64,800	64,800	64,800	64,800	648000
Total	117,640	12,8575	139,510	150,445	172,180	186,955	201,730	216,505	242,080	260,695	279,310	297,925	
Payments													
Cost of sales	27,840	2,7840	27,840	27,840	34,800	34,800	34,800	34,800	41,760	41,760	41,760	41,760	417600
Indirect costs	4,425	4,425	4,425	4,425	4,425	4,425	4,425	4,425	4,425	4,425	4,425	4,425	53100
Total	32,265	32,265	32,265	32,265	39,225	39,225	39,225	39,225	46,185	46,185	46,185	46,185	470700
Bal c/f	85,375	96,310	107,245	118,180	132,955	147,730	162,505	177,280	195,895	214,510	233,125	251,740	

Table A4.4.5 Indirect Costs for Cash Flow

	Year 1	Year 2	Year 3
Indirect costs	**2,625**	**3,525**	**4,425**
Equipment	175	175	175
Wages 1	900	900	900
Wages 2	900	1,800	2,700
Rent	300	300	300
Utilities	50	50	50
Insurance	100	100	100
Office	100	100	100
Leaflets	100	100	100

4.4 Profit and loss accounts (or income statements)

Table A4.4.6 WorldFood Enterprises Profit and Loss Accounts for the Year Ended . . . 1, 2 and 3

	Year 1 (Euros)	Year 2 (Euros)	Year 3 (Euros)
Sales	86,400	302,400	648,000
Purchases	44,160	154,560	331,200
Delivery	11,520	40,320	86,400
Cost of goods sold	55,680	194,880	417,600
Gross margin	**30,720**	**107,520**	**230,400**
Gross margin %	35.56%	35.56%	35.56%
Expenses			
Wages	21,600	32,400	43,200
Rent	3,600	3,600	3,600
Insurance	1,200	1,200	1,200
Office supplies	1,200	1,200	1,200
Utilities	600	600	600
Promotion	1,200	1,200	1,200
Miscellaneous expenses	2,004	2,004	0
Total expenses	**31,404**	**42,204**	**51,000**
Net profit before tax	**(684)**	**65,316**	**179,400**
Net profit margin before tax in %	0.79%	21.60%	27.69%
Corporation tax at 33%		21,554.28	59,202.00
Net profit after tax	**(684)**	**43,761.72**	**120,198.00**
Net profit margin after tax in %	0.79%	14.47%	18.55%

4.5 Balance Sheet

Table A4.4.7 WorldFood Enterprises Balance Sheet as at . . . Year 1, 2 and 3

	Year 1	Year 2	Year 3
Fixed assets			
Equipment	6,100	4,000	1,900
Less accumulated depreciation	(2,100)	(2,100)	(2,100)
Current assets			
Merchandise inventory	9,200	22,080	18,860
Accounts receivable	5,400	16,200	32,400
Cash	10,800	32,400	64,800
Total current assets	**25,400**	**70,680**	**116,060**
Total assets	**29,400**	**72,580**	**115,860**
Liabilities			
Accounts payable	9,200	22,080	18,860
Owner's equity	(4,800)	50,500	97,000
Capital stock	25,000	0	0
Total liabilities	**29,400**	**72,580**	**115,860**

4.6 Financial ratios

1. Profitability ratios

a. Gross profit margin = Gross profit/Sales

   1st Year: GPM = 30,720/86,400 = 35.56%
   2nd Year: GPM = 107,520/302,400 = 35.56%
   3rd Year: GPM = 230,400/648,000 = 35.56%

b. Return on investment = Net profit before tax/Capital employed

   1st Year: ROI = Nil since there is no net profit
   2nd Year: ROI = 65,316/72,580 = 89.99%
   3rd Year: ROI = 179,400/115,860 = 154.84%

2. Break-even analysis

A company's break-even point is the amount of sales or revenues that it must generate in order to equal its expenses. In other words, it is the point at which the company neither makes a profit nor suffers a loss. The formula below is used for its calculation:

BEP = Fixed total cost/(Selling price – Variable cost per unit)

For year 1, our fixed costs are 2,625 euros a month (see revenue forecast tables above). Variable cost is our buying price, plus the distribution cost: (46 + 12) euros = 58 euros/basket.

BEP = 2,625/(90 − 58) = 82
BEP = 82 units/month

We plan to acquire 40 new customers a month: 40 baskets a month is below 82. Every customer places an order every four months. In the fifth month, we will have 40 new customers, plus 40 old customers who will be placing their second order: 40 + 40 = 80 baskets a month, which is still below 82. In the ninth month, we will have 40 new customers, plus 80 old customers who will be placing another order. In this month, we will sell 120 baskets, which is above 82. We will start making profit on the ninth month of business.

5.   Operations management

5.1   Premises and layout

WorldFood will have warehouses where goods will be stocked. Delivery will depart from these warehouses. Although the customers will have the opportunity to collect their orders directly from a warehouse, our policy is home delivery. Therefore, the choice of the location is solely concerned about our delivery cost, not visibility or customers' accessibility.

5.2   Equipment

The Directors have already purchased the equipment used in the business. These include:

- a van
- a two-wheeled trolley
- office furniture
- IT equipment.

5.3   Sources of supply

We will get supply from the major food suppliers in France, such as Samia Food, Haut De Coeur, Agidra, etc. They supply most of our competitors. So as we grow, our aim is to get supply directly from the farmer, in order to offer our customers an even better price and also give ourselves a higher margin.

5.4   *Customer service*

WorldFood will offer three main customer services:

• *Delivery*

We will have a delivery system. Our customers will place their orders by phone or on the internet, and the goods will be delivered at their doorstep. The delivery system is our unique selling point, which is designed to bring about loyalty. In order to minimize the cost, this service will be organized by postcodes. The driver will deliver in a single journey to all our customers from a particular area.

• *Customer credit*

We will offer our customers payment in instalments: two or three instalments according to the volume of the order. WorldFood sells essential food commodities such as semolina, farina, rice, pasta, cooking oil and beans, etc. We will have an upselling policy so as to maximize the customer's basket, which is the total value of all the goods ordered. We expect this basket to be a minimum of 80 euros, which the customers could pay in two instalments: 50 euros on delivery (or a cheque cashable on the day or up to the end of the month) and 30 euros on a cheque to be cashed in the following month. For orders over 100 euros, three cheques could be collected.

Our customer credit policy could be qualified as easy-going, granted strict collection. As we collect all the cheques on delivery, we avoid going through all the Customer Credit Act requirements. This policy is designed to be a tool for good customer service, and it is a tool for minimizing our delivery cost. While covering a particular postcode, we can deliver to customers who don't necessarily have cash in their hand.

• *Incentives*

These incentives come from what we call an Active Word of Mouth. Therefore, they are both a customer service policy and a marketing policy. If A is our customer, we encourage A to talk about us around his/her contacts. When A1 makes a purchase through A, 2% of the order value will be credited to A's account in our books. When A11 makes a purchase through A1, 2% of the order value will be credited to A1's account, and 1% to A's account. With this Active Word of Mouth, customer A will pay less and less for his/her own orders.

6.   Human resources management

6.1   *Organizational chart/management style*

WorldFood Enterprises will adopt a democratic management style, which allows the Directors to take part in decision making. Once the business becomes successful and expands, the structure, style and culture may change to a simple structure as below. The organizational culture for WorldFood is more performance-orientated than traditional. The advantage of having a democratic style allows the business to be performance-orientated where new ideas, willingness to take on new challenges, and interdepartmental communication are encouraged.

6.2   *Key management personnel*

(i)   Managing Director – Mr Joe Paris

The Managing Director will be responsible for the long-term and strategic planning of the business. He will also be responsible for managing the day-to-day operations and for arranging for the purchase of inventories.

He holds a Master's Degree in Economics and a Postgraduate Diploma in Economics and Politics of Energy. In addition, he is a Fellow and Corporate

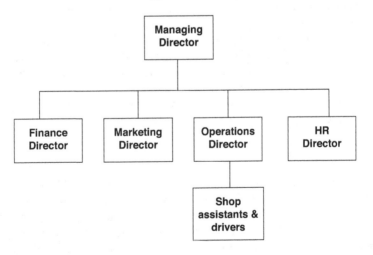

Figure A4.6.1 Organizational Chart

Member of various premier institutes – namely, the Institute of Administrative Management, the Institute of Commerce, and the Institute of Logistics and Distribution Management.

He has worked as a Manager in McDonald's in Paris. He has also worked for customer acquisition on behalf of utility companies and utility debt recovery in the UK.

(ii) Finance Director – Mrs A. Paris

The Finance Director will be responsible for the maintenance of adequate financial records. She will also be responsible for the general administration within the office and acts as a Deputy to the Managing Director when required.

She has a wide experience in office administration, having worked in a number of small businesses in the same capacity. She has a BSc in accounting and has worked as a Purchasing Manager in one of the largest purchasing groups in France.

(iii) Support workers

Other support workers include Miss B. Paris and Mr C. Klaas. Miss B. Paris has just graduated as a PR from Birmingham University. She will play a key role in the implementation of the communication and marketing strategy. Mr C. Klaas has worked as a Food Quality Controller in one of the largest catering companies in France. Both Miss B. Paris and Mr C. Klaas are co-founders and are therefore members of the Board of Directors.

6.3   Training and development

Basic continuous training will be incorporated into the company's development programme in due course, and most of the training will be in-house. The Managing Director will be responsible for designing and supervising the training programme. The training will be geared towards ways of developing and improving the quality service offered at WorldFood.

The training will also incorporate staff management, which includes improving staff morale and staff motivation by providing genuine incentives. The training pack will be designed to set high standards in providing the best service in customer acquisition, customer satisfaction, customer credit, daily books management, stock management, cash handling, lifting and handling, food hygiene, first aid etc. This includes courtesy and friendly atmosphere from staff to customers, and at the same time the efficient ways of pleasing them and understanding their needs.

There will also be standing instructions/guidance notes so that in event of any member of staff being absent (e.g. through illness), the business does not come to a standstill. Any temporary staff employed will have the aid of easily understandable instructions to work from.

6.4   *Recruitment and selection*

As the business expands, WorldFood will need to employ many categories of staff such as shop floor assistants, checkout operators and security staff who will monitor people entering and leaving the shop. The shop assistants will assist in administrative work, especially stocktaking and customer acquisition follow-up. The company will also hire a driver who will deliver orders to the customers.

6.5   *Legislation and legal compliance*

WorldFood will comply with regulations such as the Health and Safety at Work Act 1974 and the Control of Substances Hazardous to Health Act 1994 (to ensure that our premises are safe for both employees and customers) as well as the Disability Discrimination Act 1995 and the Sex Discrimination Act 1975 (to ensure that we do not discriminate against our employees on the grounds of sex or disability). We will also ensure that our premises are easily accessible to disabled people. We will comply with food hygiene regulations to ensure that food items are of the highest hygiene standard.

7.   Risk assessment

7.1   *Risk management*

The first and probably the main risk facing WorldFood Enterprises is competition. WorldFood will continue to charge competitive prices and provide good value for money in order to attract and maintain and enlarge our customer base.

The second risk for WorldFood is high staff turnover. We will continue to pay competitive salaries and wages and provide excellent working conditions to our employees.

7.2   *Exit strategy*

As an exit strategy, we will seek first and foremost to sell the business as a going concern. If the business cannot be sold as a going concern, then the owners will resort to asset stripping which involves selling the individual long-term assets of the company.

8.   Conclusion

WorldFood prides itself on its unique selling points which include high-quality food sold at slightly below competitive prices to attract customers. Our unique selling points also include Active Word of Mouth strategy, Customer Credit, and home delivery. The break-even point analysis indicates that the company will break even in the first year of operation. The financial ratios equally indicate a healthy financial position, which means that the company has sufficient sales revenue to cover operating costs right from the first year and equally healthy net profit margins in all years except the first year.

Our primary research also shows that there is a high percentage of potential customers who are interested in buying our food items and ready to patronize the business. We are convinced of our success because the directors are well-qualified with long-standing experience in retail business.

We have clearly demonstrated in our plan that we mean business in all our undertakings. We have left no stone unturned. Failing to plan is planning to fail, and we have planned to succeed in the course of our appropriate planning. Our vision is to be the vessel that brings food to all nations and to be involved in the whole food process from the farmer to the plate. Food is a basic need, and food acquisition is a challenge. We want to be part of the solution. We want to feed the nation.

Appendix 5

Sample business plan (2) – Suzan Joseph Associates Ltd

Directors
Mr Joe Blog
Mrs Su Blog

REGISTERED ADDRESS:
123 JOE BLOG ROAD
LONDON SE0 0YZ

Executive summary

Suzan Joseph Associates (SJA) Ltd is a property development company. It is intended that the business will serve the South East of London to start with and the whole of London and beyond in due course.

Our aim is to provide very high-quality homes to customers. We aim to be the best by providing a flourishing working environment for our employees in the future. We also aim at putting something back into our local community, as our establishment will contribute to rural regeneration.

The business will initially be operating from the home of the directors located at 123 Joe Blog Road, London SE0 0YZ.

The projected profit and loss account shows that the business will be profitable from year 1. The net profit in the first year of operation is expected to be £196,260 before tax.

The legal status of the company is a Limited Company, and it is owned by two directors – namely:

Mr Joe Blog   –   Managing Director
Mrs Su Blog   –   Finance Director

This business plan may be used for the purpose of obtaining financial assistance from banks and may also be presented to other financial institutions for such purposes.

Contents

Executive summary

1. Introduction

- Business history
- Business name
- Legal form

2. Business strategy

- Vision
- Mission statement
- Aims and objectives
- SWOT analysis
- Location
- Directors names and addresses

3. Marketing/market research

- Market size
- Target market
- Competitors
- Primary research analysis
- Advertising and promotion strategies
- Selling strategies

4. Finance

- Start-up costs
- Gearing
- Payments by clients
- Projected cash flow
- Projected profit and loss account
- Balance sheet
- Break-even analysis YR1, YR2
- Other finance ratios

5. Operations management

- Premises
- Equipment
- Sources of supply
- Operations process

6. **Human resources management**

    - Organizational chart/management style
    - Key people and their function
    - Training and development
    - Recruitment and selection
    - Legislation and legal compliance

7. **Risk assessment**

    - Risk management
    - Exit strategy

8. **Conclusion**

1.   Introduction

1.1   Business history

SJA is a property-developing business. Our main activities shall include buying undeveloped or run-down properties and building them up and selling them on. As this occurs, great value is added to the developed property, and thus there is a potential for high profits and quick return on capital. This plan will be used to assist Suzan Joseph Associates Ltd in securing the required start-up capital from financial institutions.

We have a wealth of experience in property development which will put us in a position to generate huge income. Firstly, economic conditions are quite favourable for the property industry in the UK and also in many places around the world. There is currently huge demand for housing in the UK, despite rapidly rising property prices. The industry is relatively stable in the sense that there will always be demand for housing; therefore, we believe that we will successfully be able to sell our properties. Secondly, although sales will be few in number to start with, each individual sale represents a significant amount of profits earned.

We have explored and identified potential customers through market research. Our market research shows that the South East of London contains a large population of people, such as professionals and working-class citizens. We believe that property development will benefit the local community, as they would be provided with an opportunity to obtain quality, brand-new houses at prices which are lower than usual in the area. We feel that the main people who would benefit from our business would be young couples and other first-time buyers, as it is more difficult for them to be able to get their foot on the first rung of the property ladder due to high prices. They would, we believe, benefit from our houses, which would be sold at affordable prices.

Apart from the sale of properties, we intend in due course to retain ownership of some properties and to let them out, thus providing us with additional stable income.

1.2 Business name

The name of the business is Suzan Joseph Associates (SJA) Limited.

1.3 Legal form

The business will be incorporated as a Limited Liability Company. As a Limited Liability Company, the liability of the Directors and potential shareholders is limited to the amount of capital that each of them has invested in the company. This form of incorporation will make the company more attractive to banks and other investors. The downside to this is the need to comply with more regulations and greater disclosure of information.

2. Business strategy

2.1 Vision

The vision of the company is to improve the quality of life of the people by providing them with high-quality homes and by making our impact felt in the local community.

2.2 Mission statement

Our aim is to provide very high-quality homes to people. We aim to be the best by providing a flourishing working environment for our employees in the future. We also aim at putting something back into our local community.

2.3 Aims and objectives

Short-term objectives

- To gain a foothold in the UK property market by successfully developing and selling our first property.
- To establish a good reputation among customers and to excel in customer satisfaction.
- To gain a competitive edge over rival property developers.
- To be able to pay off our loan capital as quickly as possible.

Long-term objectives

- To expand within the UK market and become an established and well-known property developer in the next ten years.
- To diversify our developments to all varieties of property (flats, houses, office buildings etc.).
- To increase our customer base by at least 20% each year.
- To develop a sustainable and profitable business.
- To expand to other geographical areas as well as expand our investment in the business.
- To develop properties abroad by the year 2012.

2.4   SWOT analysis

Table A5.2.1 Showing a SWOT Analysis

Strengths	Weaknesses
• Strong management team • High-quality properties • Lack of competitors in the operating area • Well-qualified and experienced directors • Little amount spent on advertisement • Profitable from the first year • Available local estate agents	• Operating from home, although this is also a strength • High property prices • High interest rates
Opportunities	**Threats**
• Possibility to expand to other areas • Possibility to develop staff skills and knowledge through training courses • Opportunity to add new products (e.g. flats)	• Future competition • Unstable interest rates • Too many government regulations and legislation

2.5   Location

The business is located at 123 Joe Blog Road, London SE0 0YZ. Initially, the business will be conducted from home, as an office is not required at this stage. This is due to lack of finance during start-up. However, once we have successfully progressed through the market, we will consider setting up an office, which will be more suitable for business activities as well as able to accommodate employees.

2.6   Directors names and addresses

Mr Joe Blog – Managing Director: 123 Joe Blog Road, London SE0 0YZ.
Mrs Su Blog – Finance Director: 123 Joe Blog Road, London SE0 0YZ.

3.   Marketing/market research

3.1   Nature of market

The UK house-building market is extremely large, but there has been a rapid growth since last year. Although there is expected to be a slight fall in the property market in the coming years, it is expected not to crash but to be on hold for a short period of time. However, house prices have been increasing over the past few years and are expected to do so in the future. Thus, we have the potential to sell our houses at average prices successfully. We will begin the business by purchasing a run-down property and refurbishing it, which is expected to take between three to six months. By the time the refurbishment is completed, we will have advertised and promoted the property using an extensive marketing strategy. The two Directors are motivated and determined to sell the property to the right customers. There will always be a demand for high-quality homes, and we are confident that we will succeed.

The housing market is volatile at the moment due to increasingly high interest rates, and thus households face higher mortgages. Interest rates are currently at 6.5%. The rise in interest rates has led to an increase in house prices, but people are still willing to purchase properties as they tend to feel safer knowing they own the property rather than rent it. Although this rise in interest rates means customers face higher debts and thus more stress, they are not put off by it. The housing market is booming and is still growing and so we have the potential to sell our properties at reasonable prices.

The UK economy is doing well, and there is expected to be strong growth throughout the next few years. The strong economy will help us with our business as it helps support the housing market. If interest rates rise to over 7%, then there is likely to be a downfall in house prices, but this is not predicted to happen, and so it will not affect the success of our business.

3.2   Competitor analysis

Although London is seemingly well served with property developers, we do not have direct competitors at the moment in the Eltham area. However, it is likely that when the business starts to make supernormal profits, other firms will enter the market to compete for a share of the market.

3.3   Unique selling point

Our unique selling point is that we will be providing high-quality homes and selling them at slightly below the competitive market price to attract first-time buyers. Although our research indicated that 77% of these people prefer their property to be unfurnished (see 3.5 below), we intend to supply our customers with the major necessary appliances in the household as an incentive.

Our houses will conform to government standards for new buildings. They will be seen as unique and affordable to potential customers. We will differentiate ourselves and gain a competitive advantage through offering customers attractive, quality homes at suitable prices and with good parking facilities where possible.

3.4   Target market

We are aiming to sell the houses to the target market of the middle and skilled working class. We hope to attract young couples who are first time buyers and who want to buy an affordable home without increasing their debts too much. This is why our unique selling point of selling below the competitive market price will be attractive to our target market.

3.5   Primary research analysis

In our primary research, 1,000 people were questioned about their buying intentions. They were asked if they intended to buy a house in the next 24 months: 80% of them said 'yes', while only 20% indicated that they had no such intention. This shows a very high proportion of potential buyers.

Table A5.3.1 Buying Intentions

	Yes	No
Purchase within 24 months	80%	20%
Purchased before	75%	25%

When asked whether they had purchased property before, 75% of them said 'no', while 25% said that they had purchased a house before. Again, this shows a high proportion of potential first-time buyers. Potential customers were also asked whether they would prefer their house to be furnished or not: 77% of them indicated that they would like to furnish their houses by themselves and to their own taste.

Interviewees were asked about the type of property they are interested in buying: 35% of respondents were interested in terrace or end-of-terrace houses, 30% in flats, 20% in semi-detached houses, and 15% in fully detached houses. Understandably, as first-time buyers, they would want to get on the property ladder by starting with less-expensive properties.

Table A5.3.2 Type of Property

Type	%
Terraced	35%
Semi-detached	20%
Fully detached	15%
Flat	30%
Total	100%

Interestingly, 70% of the respondents were male, while 30% were female. Respondents were also asked about their marital status: 20% of them indicated they were single, 30% indicated that they were not legally married but were living with a partner, while half of them were married couples as shown in the table below.

Table A5.3.3 Marital Status

Status	%
Single	20%
Cohabiting	30%
Married	50%

Finally, respondents were asked if they would be willing to pay more money for an eco-friendly house/flat. An overwhelming majority (80%) indicated that they would not like to pay more for eco-friendly houses, while only 20% said they would like to pay more for it as shown below. Therefore, the company will not necessarily pursue an eco-friendly strategy. However, because the houses will be built to comply with British regulatory requirements, they will be not only energy efficient but also environmentally friendly.

3.6   *Promotion and advertising*

SJA will promote and advertise properties by using various methods of advertising to attract potential customers. We have set ourselves an advertising budget of £5,000 for the first three houses we hope to sell. We will advertise our properties through construction site boards, websites, *estate agents* and local newspapers. These advertising methods will allow us to find the right customers for the properties.

3.7   *Sales and pricing*

We intend to sell at least one property per quarter, and therefore we intend to use an extensive marketing strategy, taking into account the marketing mix to ensure we sell the three houses in the first year of operation as quickly as possible. The marketing strategy will take into account the fact that we aim to meet the target market of the middle and skilled working class. Our properties are aimed at young working couples who are first-time property buyers.

We will be conducting penetration pricing in order to ensure we sell all of the properties immediately once they are ready. The houses will be sold at below the competitive market price as this is our unique selling point and is guaranteed to attract customers to our business. Selling at lower prices than expected by customers will allow us to make successful sales and to satisfy our customers and thus strengthen and build our brand image. Our asking price for the houses will be in the region of £200,000, and we are confident we can sell them at this price.

4.   Finance

4.1   Start-up costs

To start up, the company needs a minimum of £400,000, which is to be used in the following areas:

- purchase of three run-down properties for £200,000 total
- hiring a construction company to build the properties, expected to cost £150,000 (£50,000 per house)
- overhead expenses, estimated to be £50,000.

4.2   Gearing

The two directors in the venture have already invested about £5,000 of their money by way of computer equipment and other fixtures and fittings, whereas the remaining capital is expected to be raised from a bank loan. Even though this capital mix will result in a high gearing ratio for the company to start with, there is no risk whatsoever for the lenders. This is because the capital will be invested on tangible assets; therefore, the risk for the bank losing its money would be reduced considerably as it can repossess the properties if the company defaults in complying with the payment terms and conditions of the loan.

4.3   Payments by clients

Our solicitors will handle all payments and will remit all monies due to us into our bank account. They will also deal with all conveyance matters.

4.4   Projected cash flow

The cash flow forecast shown below is projected from estimated quarterly sales of £600,000. It is assumed that the figures in the cash flow (both receipts and payments) will be relatively stable for at least the first year. In

Table A5.4.1 Suzan Joseph Associates Ltd Cash Flow Forecast for the Period 01/01/XXXX – 31/12/XXXX

	Jan	Feb	Mar	Apr	May	Jun	Jul	Aug	Sep	Oct	Nov	Dec	Total
	£	£	£	£	£	£	£	£	£	£	£	£	£
Receipts													
Sales				200,000				200,000				200,000	**600,000**
Capital investment	5,000	0	0	0	0	0	0	0	0	0	0	0	**5,000**
Loan	400,000	0	0	0	0	0	0	0	0	0	0	0	**400000**
Total receipts (A)	**405,000**	**0**	**0**	**200,000**	**0**	**0**	**0**	**200,000**	**0**	**0**	**0**	**200,000**	**1,005,000**
Payments													
Rent	500	500	500	500	500	500	500	500	500	500	500	500	**6,000**
Advertising	1,250	0	1,250	0	0	0	1,250	0	0	0	1,250	0	**5,000**
Legal fees	0	0	0	2,333	0	0	0	2,333	0	0	0	2,334	**7,000**
Lighting and heating	0	0	600	0	0	600	0	0	600	0	0	600	**2,400**
Telephone	0	0	600	0	0	600	0	0	600	0	0	600	**2,400**
Equipment purchase	5,000	0	0	0	0	0	0	0	0	0	0	0	**5,000**
Postage/stationery	20	20	20	20	20	20	20	20	20	20	20	20	**240**
Purchases of property	66,666	0	0	0	66,667	0	0	0	66,667	0	0	0	**200,000**
Planning permission	666	0	0	0	667	0	0	0	667	0	0	0	**2,000**
Interest on loan	2,300	2,300	2,300	2,300	2,300	2,300	2,300	2,300	2,300	2,300	2,300	2,300	**27,600**
Bank charges	50	50	50	50	50	50	50	50	50	50	50	50	**600**
Total payments (B)	**76,452**	**2,870**	**5,320**	**5,203**	**70,204**	**4,070**	**4,120**	**5,203**	**71,404**	**2,870**	**4,120**	**6,404**	**258,240**
Cash balances													
Cash flow (A − B)	**328,548**	**-2,870**	**-5,320**	**194,797**	**-70,204**	**-4,070**	**-4,120**	**194,797**	**-71,404**	**-2,870**	**-4,120**	**193,596**	**746,760**
Opening balance	0	328,548	325,678	320,358	515,155	444,951	440,881	436,761	631,558	560,154	557,284	553,164	
Closing balance	328,548	325,678	320,358	515,155	444,951	440,881	436,761	631,558	560,154	557,284	553,164	746,760	

year 2, it is assumed that at least four properties will be sold and that there will be a 5% increase in the price of properties. It is also assumed that the cost of dilapidated properties and construction costs will increase by 2%, interest rate will increase to 7%, while other expenses will remain constant.

4.5 Projected profit and loss account

Table A5.4.2 Suzan Joseph Associates Ltd Profit and Loss Account for the Year Ended 31/12/XXX1

	£	£
Sales	600,000	
Purchases	200,000	
Construction	*150,000*	
Cost of sales	*350,000*	
Gross profit	250,000	
Less expenses		
Telephone bills	2,400	
Rent	6,000	
Lighting and heating	2,400	
Planning permission expenses	2,000	
Advertising	5,000	
Legal fees	7,000	
Postage/stationery	240	
Interest on loan (at 6.9% APR)	27,600	
Bank charges	600	
Depreciation	500	
Total expenses		*53,740*
Net profit		196,260
Less corporation tax (20%)		*39,252*
Profit after tax		157,008
Appropriation of profit		
Drawings		*60,000*
Reserves		*97,008*

Table A5.4.3 Suzan Joseph Associates Ltd Profit and Loss Account for the Year Ended 31/12/XXX2

	£	£
Sales		840,000
Purchase of properties	272,000	
Construction	*153,000*	
Cost of sales		*425,000*
Gross profit		415,000

	£	£
Less expenses		
Telephone bills	2,400	
Rent	6,000	
Lighting and heating	2,400	
Planning permission expenses	2,000	
Advertising	5,000	
Legal fees	7,000	
Postage/stationery	240	
Interest on loans (at 7% APR)	33,250	
Bank charges	600	
Depreciation	*500*	
Total expenses		*59,390*
Net profit		355,610
Less corporation tax (20%)		*72,252*
Profit after Tax		283,358
Appropriation of profit		
Drawings		*60,000*
Reserves		*223,358*

4.6   Balance sheet

Table A5.4.4 Suzan Joseph Associates Ltd Balance Sheet as at 31/12/XXX1

	£	£
Fixed assets		
Computers		3,000
Printers/photocopying Machine		1,000
Fixtures and fittings		1,000
Less depreciation		*(500)*
Net fixed assets		4,500
Current assets		
Cash at bank	196,260	
Less current liabilities		
Corporation tax	*39,252*	*157,008*
Net worth		161,508
Financed by		
Capital	4,500	
Reserves	97,008	
Drawings	*60,000*	
Shareholders' funds		*161,508*

4.7   Break-even analysis YR1, YR2

Break-even sales: Fixed costs + Net profit/Gross profit margin

YR1		
4,500 + 196,260/0.42	£478,000	
YR2		
4,000 + 355,610/0.49		£733,898

3.8   Other financial ratios

(i)   Gross profit % = *Gross profit/Sales*

YR1		
Gross profit = 250,000		
Sales = 600,000	42%	
YR2		
Gross profit = 415,000		
Sales = 840,000		49%

(ii)   Net profit margin = *Net profit/Sales*

YR1		
Net profit = 196,260		
Sales = 600,000	33%	
YR2		
Net profit = 355,610		
Sales = 840,000		42%

(iii) Interest over = *Operating profit/Interest charges*

YR1		
Operating profit = 250,000		
Interest charge = 27,600	9 times	12 times
YR2		
Operating profit = 415,000		
Interest charge = 33,250		

The forecasts clearly show that the business will succeed in the market. From the initial investment of £400,000 in year 1, the company expects to generate a turnover of £600,000 in the same year, of which £196,260 is expected to be net profit before tax. The net profit margin ratio clearly shows 33% of the company's sales. In other words, 33 pence of every pound generated from sales will be net profit. The year 2 forecast shows that this ratio improves even further to 42%.

Interest is covered 9 times in year 1 and 12 times in year 2, which means that the business will be able to meet its debts out of earnings and can be considered as a satisfactory risk by creditors. The breakeven of £478,000 shows the level of activity where the business is likely to produce neither profit nor loss; thus, the business will break even in the first year of operation.

5. Operations management

5.1 Premises

The directors of SJA will operate the business from home, which is located at 123 Joe Blog Road, London SE0 0YZ. The premises are strategically located near Eltham High Street and also near estate agents and many shops and banks on the High Street. The business charge for the rent of the premises is £500 per month (£6,000 per annum).

The property is free-hold and owned by the Directors. It is properly maintained and fully insured.

5.2 Equipment

The Directors have already spent £5,000 on the purchase of the equipment used in the business. These include:

- computer and software – £3,000
- printers and photocopier – £1,000
- fixture and fittings – £1,000.

5.3 Sources of supply

There are many estate agents open to SJA, but we will use those whose properties are reasonable in terms of prices. Every effort will be made to ensure that expenditure on run-down properties is prudent and kept to a minimum.

5.4 Operations process

When a potentially useful plot of land or dilapidated property has been found, the first step is to get surveyors to inspect the land/property to see if it is suitable for development. The surveyors will study the geographical properties of the land, such as slopes and soil density, and advise on what can be built and where. The architecture team will then design the building, taking into consideration the information from the surveyors. The architects must also take into account requirements from the local council, in order to successfully obtain planning permission.

Once planning permission is obtained and all the plans have been laid out, we shall purchase the plot of land/property. From this point onwards, most of the work will be carried out by construction contractors, while our role shifts more to marketing, i.e. selling the properties. We shall also supervise the construction works in order to make sure that everything is going as planned and on schedule or ahead of schedule if possible. The construction process itself should take no more than six months, depending on the speed of the workers, weather conditions or other unforeseen circumstances.

The finished products will be homes, which will be sold to customers through estate agents. The two Directors of Suzan Joseph Associates will be responsible for managing the day-to-day operations of the development.

6.   Human resources management

6.1   *Organizational chart/management style*

Suzan Joseph Associates will adopt a democratic management style, which allows the Directors to take part in decision making. Once the business becomes successful and expands, the structure, style and culture may change to a simple structure as below. The organizational culture for Suzan Joseph Associates is more performance-orientated than traditional. The advantage of having a democratic style allows the business to be performance-orientated where new ideas, willingness to take on new challenges, and interdepartmental communication are encouraged.

6.2   *Key management personnel*

(i)   *Managing Director – Mr Joe Blog*

The Managing Director will be responsible for the long-term and strategic planning of the business. He will also be responsible for managing the day-to-day operations and for arranging for the purchase of properties to be developed.

He holds a Diploma in Business Studies, a Postgraduate Diploma in Estate Management, and an MBA. In addition, he is a Fellow and Corporate Member of various premier institutes – namely: the National Association of Estate Agents, the Institute of Administrative Management, the Institute of Commerce, and the Institute of Logistics and Distribution Management.

(ii)   Finance Director – Mrs Su Blog

The Finance Director will be responsible for the maintenance of adequate financial records. She will also be responsible for the general administration within the office and acts as a Deputy to the Managing Director when required.

She has wide experience in office administration, having worked in a number of property development companies. She has an MBA from South Bank University, and she is also a Fellow of the Institute of Cost and Executive Accountants.

6.3   Training and development

Basic continuous training will be incorporated into the company's development programme in due course, and most of the training will be in-house. The Managing Director will be responsible for designing and supervising the training programme. The training will be geared towards ways of developing and improving the quality service offered at Suzan Joseph Associates. The training will also incorporate staff management, which includes improving staff morale and staff motivation by providing genuine incentives. The training pack will be designed to set high standards in providing the best service in the property development business. This includes courtesy and friendly atmosphere from staff to customers, and at the same time the efficient ways of pleasing them and understanding their needs.

There will also be standing instructions/guidance notes so that in the event of any member of staff being absent (e.g. through illness), the business does not come to a standstill. Any temporary staff employed will have the aid of easily understandable instructions to work from.

6.4   Recruitment and selection

SJA will need to contract jobs out to builders, plumbers and electricians to carry out the internal work and the external foundations of each property. There will be many people on-site doing various jobs, and, for safety reasons, a log will be kept of people entering and leaving the site.

6.5   Legislation and legal compliance

Complying with the building regulations under the Building Act 1984 is of great importance to ensure standards are met for the design and building, as well as complying with the Health and Safety at Work Act 1974. The responsibility usually lies with the builder.

Energy Performance Certificates will be required for our properties, and a certificate will be given which illustrates advice of energy efficiency and further improvements that can be made. As from 2009, all properties that are bought, sold or let must have the certificate.

Building regulations (2004) and amendments (2006) will be complied with to ensure the health and safety of people around building. This involves construction, drainage, ventilation and sound insulation. Any building project must comply with building regulations. The Building Act 1984 falls under building regulations and covers conservation of fuel and power, preventing waste, and protecting the environment.

Building regulations approval will be obtained either by giving full plans to the local authority or by giving a building notice to the local authority, and in many cases fees may need to be paid. Other regulations to comply with include the Health and Safety at Work Act 1974, Control of Substances Hazardous to Health Act 1994, Disability Discrimination Act 1995, and Sex Discrimination Act 1975.

7.   Risk assessment

7.1   Risk management

The first and probably the main risk facing Suzan Joseph Associates is charging clients high fees which can prevent potential clients from using our products and services. SJA will continue to provide good value for money in order to attract and maintain its clientele.

The second risk for SJA is losing trained members of staff who move on to establish their own business to compete with us. SJA will continue to pay competitive salaries and wages and provide excellent working conditions to its employees.

7.2   Exit strategy

As an exit strategy, SJA will seek first and foremost to sell the business as a going concern. If the business cannot be sold as a going concern, then the owners will resort to asset stripping, which involves selling the individual long-term assets of the company.

8.   Conclusion

The Managing Director of SJA is seeking a four-year loan in the amount of £400,000 to be repaid at a fixed interest rate of 7% each year with a monthly payment of £8,917. This loan will be secured on the personal property of the Managing Director, which is valued at £500,000.

SJA prides itself in its unique selling point, which is high-quality homes sold at slightly below competitive prices to attract first-time buyers. The break-even point analysis indicates that the company will break even in the first year of operation. Other financial ratios equally indicate a healthy financial position, which means that the company has sufficient sales revenue to cover operating costs right from the first year and equally healthy net profit margins in both years. The interest cover also demonstrates the company's ability to make interest payments on its debts on time.

Our primary research also shows that there is a high percentage of potential clients who are interested in buying property in the area and ready to patronize the business. We are convinced of our success because the Directors are well-qualified with long-standing experience in property development and estate management.

We have clearly demonstrated in our plan that the business will succeed in all ramifications.

Appendix 6
An example of a mission statement

"McDonald's brand mission is to be our customers' favourite place and way to eat and drink. Our worldwide operations are aligned around a global strategy called the Plan to Win, which centre on an exceptional customer experience – People, Products, Place, Price and Promotion. We are committed to continuously improving our operations and enhancing our customers' experience."

Appendix 7

An example of a vision statement

"McDonald's vision is to be the world's best quick service restaurant experience. Being the best means providing outstanding quality, service, cleanliness, and value, so that we make every customer in every restaurant smile."

Index

Printed in the United States
by Baker & Taylor Publisher Services